Heather's
Rage

Heather's Rage

A Mother's Faith Reflected in Her Daughter's Mental Illness

BY LESLIE BYERS

BROWN BOOKS PUBLISHING GROUP

HEATHER'S RAGE: A MOTHER'S FAITH REFLECTED
IN HER DAUGHTER'S MENTAL ILLNESS
© 2004 By Leslie Byers

Manufactured in the United States of America.

For information, please contact:
Brown Books Publishing Group
16200 North Dallas Parkway, Suite 170
Dallas, Texas 75248
www.brownbooks.com
972-381-0009
ISBN: 0-9753907-1-6
LCCN: 2004094193

Table of Contents

Acknowledgements

This book could not have been possible without the encouragement and support of many people.

To my colleagues at the Omaha World-Herald—whose writing and editing skills, along with their friendship, enabled me to accomplish my goals. I know it is providence that led me to this newspaper since I was not a writer by trade before setting out to write this book. Simply being around them and watching them perfect their craft was an inspiration for me to accept nothing less than the best.

Larry King, executive editor—whose professional wisdom and encouragement spurred me to continue when, at times, I was ready to give up.

Deanna Sands, managing editor—whose advice early on took a very rough draft and infused new light into it.

Sue Truax, copy desk editor—whose writing and editing skills, along with her personal insight, gave me the emotional and technical support that I needed and without which I could not have completed this book.

Jim Johnson, copy editor—who, with a sleight of pen, can change one word that suddenly makes a sentence come alive.

Michael Kelly, columnist—whose style I aspired to measure up to because he always captures the true spirit of people in his writing.

To Rebecca Rotert and Chandra Sparks Taylor—for their literary expertise.

To my dear friend Steve Szmrecsanyi—who from the beginning was a big part of my writing and his advice was invaluable. I regret that he passed away before this came to completion, but his spirit is very much a part of the book.

To the fantastic people of Brown Books: Milli Brown—President; Kathryn Grant—Editorial Director; Deepa Pillai—Editor; Alyson Alexander—Creative Director; Erica Jennings—Designer; Heather Horton—Cover artwork; Troy Smith—Line editor; and Deanne Dice—Proofreader.

To my children—without their love and support this would have been all for naught. My children are such a wonderful blessing to me. They have taught me and shown me how to love in ways I never thought possible.

And to my husband—whose enduring love, support, patience, and friendship has made my life fuller than I ever imagined.

WHEN YOU COME TO THE EDGE

OF ALL THE LIGHT YOU KNOW

AND ARE ABOUT TO STEP OFF

INTO THE DARKNESS OF THE UNKNOWN—

FAITH IS THE CONSCIOUS AWARENESS THAT ONE

OF TWO THINGS WILL HAPPEN:

THERE WILL BE SOMETHING SOLID TO STAND ON,

OR YOU WILL BE TAUGHT HOW TO FLY.

—Author Unknown

Author's Notes

With the exception of my husband and me, the names of characters have been changed. It is unfortunate but necessary, because the very reason I am writing this book—to help shed the stigma associated with mental illness—is the very reason others names have been changed—to protect them from the shame still associated with mental illness. It is my hope that someday mental illness will no longer be considered shameful but rather a courageous journey to be conquered.

Introduction

Life is a journey, not a destination. Most of us go through life following a carefully-planned route. But on my journey I learned that the roads we take can be fraught with unexpected detours. My family faced such a detour, which took us on a path quite different from the world we knew and turned our lives inside out.

Our precarious path took us down the road of a mental illness called bipolar disorder. Bipolar is a mood disorder. Our moods affect the temperature of our emotions and powerfully influence the way we think and act. But sometimes moods go awry. And when they do, they alter our perception of reality.

At a very young age, my daughter, Heather, began to manifest symptoms of extreme behavior that was later diagnosed as bipolar, also referred to as manic depression because of the associated states of mania and depression. Her behavior ranged from euphoria, delusion, irrational anger, and impulsive actions with absolutely no consideration for consequences, to extreme volatility and depressive lows that sometimes resulted in attempts of suicide. Fortunately, Heather's attempts were not successful, but the guilt and anguish they left are nonetheless painful.

In addition to Heather, my family includes my husband, Steve, and our two sons, Michael and Mark. Without their love and support and my faith, I doubt that I could have come through this experience intact. This story I share as the mother of a child with bipolar is a love story between Heather and me—a love that was strained because I seemed to be the target of her aggression.

My family is a Christian one of average means. Yet in order to overcome the problems Heather's illness presented, we had to draw on strength from within that we never knew we possessed. My husband and I had to support our family while dealing with the effects of this illness on our lives. We had to work with school systems inadequately equipped to deal with the severity of Heather's behavior and to learn the rules of the mental health and juvenile court systems. Most of all, we strived to maintain some semblance of a normal family life.

My struggle with Heather's illness also involved a struggle with my faith. Raising a child with bipolar has been an experience that has tried all my energy, faith, knowledge, patience, kindness, and love. For many years, I struggled to understand why God would allow such a terrible illness to befall my little girl and cause such anguish for my family.

Heather and I spent many hours discussing this book. We hope that in revealing the details of her attacks of mania, depression, and psychosis, others with similar situations will not feel alone or ashamed of what they are experiencing. I hope the sharing of this journey will shed some light on the nature of this illness, in order to replace ignorance with an understanding of this extreme disorder, which Penelope Parker, author and bipolar patient, describes as "a roller-coaster existence, ascending into heaven sometimes and then descending into hell." Above all, I wish to replace despair with hope!

I did not volunteer for this experience, anticipating instead a simpler life ministering to the gentle needs of my children. But through this experience I have gained a deeper awareness of God's love and what is really important in our relationships and acceptance of one another.

Any journey in life will have defining moments that shape who and what we are and leave us with knowledge and skills that we never imagined. For me, the value of that knowledge is diminished if I do not share it with others so that our experience can lead to discovery and recovery for someone else. If this book awakens that knowledge, strength, and reassurance for even one person, one family, then Heather and I have achieved our goal.

Part One:
Our Darkest Day

June 5, 1996

June 5, 1996, lives in my memory as one of the worst days of my life. Heather, my ten-year-old daughter, had just awakened and was obviously in one of her moods. She was surly and angry and was not afraid to let everyone know it.

She stomped to the bathroom, slamming down each foot, making sure each new step landed harder and louder than the last. When she entered the bathroom, she shut the door with such force that it violently shook the house. I tried to ignore her banging around and even hoped it would help get Michael, my thirteen-year-old son, out of bed.

As I stood at the kitchen counter buttering my toast, I heard Heather scream from the bathroom. "Why isn't there any damn hot water!"

I silently prayed, *Please, God, don't let her get out of control today!*

My husband, Steve, and my younger son, Mark, were not home. Mark, a second grader, had already caught the school bus, and Steve had just left for work. With Heather's surly mood, I pondered the wisdom of my earlier statement to Steve: "Don't worry about going in early. I can get Heather to school by myself."

I was not surprised by Heather's mood. After all, my family had been dealing with her extreme behavior since she was just a toddler. As she got older, the volatile mood swings occurred with much more intensity and frequency. Dealing with her explosive behavior was becoming a daily ordeal for my family.

I moved to the foot of the stairs and yelled at Michael to get out of bed, but he did not stir. Just then Heather came out of the bathroom and stomped back into her room. I dared to ask her, "Heather, are you almost ready for school?"

She yelled, "I'm not going to school! There's no hot water, and I'm not going anywhere without washing my hair."

My body tensed as I prepared for her impending rage.

Heather continued to stomp around her bedroom. Periodically, she turned up her music, a little louder each time—the level matching her anger. I hoped Heather would calm down without my interference but eventually, exasperated, I walked upstairs to her room to ask her to turn down the music. As I reached her doorway, she slammed the door in my face, missing my nose by a hair. I opened the door, and she immediately yelled, "Who the hell said you could come in my room?"

I was livid and responded, "I'm your mother, that's who— and I will come in your room if I need to. Turn the music down."

Heather retorted, "I'll turn it down when I want to." With this response, I entered her room, snatched the radio plug out of the wall and took the radio away from her. She jumped from her bed in an attempt to get her radio back. I pulled back just before she could grab it.

Angered by her unsuccessful attempt to retrieve her radio, Heather flew into a rage. She ran out of her bedroom and downstairs to the living room, screaming every expletive she knew. And believe me, she knew them all.

Once in the living room, she picked up one of the small chairs and hurled it across the room, hitting the entertainment center with such force that one of the chair legs split in half. Then she grabbed the floor lamp and slammed it against the wall—the glass from the globe shattering into tiny pieces everywhere. I ran to her and tried to stop her. She punched me in the stomach, landing a blow that nearly took my breath away.

In desperation, I called out to Michael upstairs, but he was sound asleep and did not hear me. I ran for the phone in the kitchen and dialed 911.

I pleaded to the dispatcher, "Please send an officer to take my daughter to the hospital; she is out of control. She's breaking things and hitting me."

Hearing my pleas, Heather ran back upstairs into her bedroom. Her tirade continued. I could hear her throwing things against her bedroom wall, and the sound of the wood giving way as she repeatedly kicked the door.

Within five minutes, an officer arrived. He needed no introduction because he had been to our house many times in the past; he knew of our family and the circumstances. He spent little time assessing the volatility of the situation. As he approached the living room, he heard Heather screaming and banging on the walls in her bedroom.

I called to Heather from the bottom of the stairs, "Heather, calm down and come down here!"

Unaware of the sheriff's presence, she ignored me. Instead she went to Michael's room and yelled, "Michael, will you kill Mom?"

I looked at the sheriff in stunned disbelief.

Michael asked Heather, "What did you say?"

Heather repeated, "Will you kill Mom?"

I could not believe Heather could even think of such words, yet they were said.

The sheriff said to me, "That's it. I'm taking her to jail." He was, of course, referring to juvenile detention, but in my mind there was no difference. Jail or juvenile detention meant Heather would be locked up among criminals, with little chance for treatment.

As he started up the stairs, I grabbed him by the arm and pleaded, "No, please don't do that. Heather didn't mean it. She needs help, not jail!"

Though Heather's words were terribly painful, I did not think she had the capacity to carry out her threats. I knew they were exaggerated words fueled by her manic-induced rage—rage brought on by improperly treated mental illness—but the officer was not convinced that she would not act upon them.

He said to me, "I am not going to come to this house again to find someone dead. She is going to jail."

I pleaded, "Jail will only do her more harm." I explained that Heather was being treated for mental illness and that she was on the waiting list for a residential treatment center. I asked him to call Emily, Heather's caseworker.

The sheriff called Emily from the phone in the kitchen. Emily asked him to take Heather to the residential treatment center downtown while she requested placement through an emergency petition. Even though Emily made the request, there were no guarantees that Heather would be placed that day, so it was possible she would spend the night in jail.

Standing at the top of the stairs, Heather overheard the entire conversation between the sheriff and Emily. I looked at her, trying to gauge her demeanor. I gently asked her to come downstairs. I did not expect Heather to obey. Frankly, I thought she would become more combative when she realized where she was being taken. But, thankfully, she came downstairs—calmly and quietly. I tried to understand what she was feeling. I knew she had to be scared, but she would not show it. I reached out to her, but she pushed me away.

The sheriff asked me to ride in the cruiser with them to the treatment center. I accepted his offer and quickly ran upstairs to dress and call into work to let them know I would not be there. I stuffed a few of Heather's belongings in an overnight bag. I figured I could come back later once I found out what she needed—that is, if she were placed in the treatment center. If she went to jail, she wouldn't need much. As I hurried around the house grabbing a few things Heather might need, I prayed fervently that God would direct the events of this day for the best possible outcome for Heather and my family.

Please, God. We really need your help right now.

Upon our arrival at the treatment center, an administrator told us to wait in the lobby while Emily's request was reviewed. I sat in a chair in the corner. As the first hour passed, the wait was agonizing. Another hour went by before the administrator came out for more information. She told me that placement was likely, but I could not relax until it was confirmed. I could not stand the thought of Heather in jail, but the sheriff made it very clear that if Heather did not get accepted into the treatment center she was going to jail. I kept thinking, *They've got to see she needs help!*

Finally, after another thirty minutes, we were informed that Heather would be admitted. The administrator asked us to wait a little longer while the paperwork was completed. Fifteen minutes later, Emily arrived to escort Heather into the treatment center.

The administrator directed us inside and locked the steel doors behind us. As the lock snapped into place, Heather jumped. A staff member came to take Heather to her room. She resisted at first, but when she realized she had no choice, she begrudgingly complied. With slumped shoulders, she followed the staff member down the hall, never once looking back at me. Time stood still as I watched her walk down the hall and round the corner. I bit my lip to contain the cries that were ready to explode from my chest.

Why, I silently asked myself, *is this happening to my little girl?*

The administrator motioned for me to follow her to the office. Immediately I was barraged with questions, forms, and instructions. I struggled to respond and just wanted to go into a corner and cry.

The intake evaluations during Heather's previous hospitalizations were intrusive, but these questions went far deeper into the intimate details of our lives. They wanted to know how much money my husband and I made, if we drank, and if we were happily married—information I preferred to keep private. As the stream of questions continued, I began to feel uncomfortable—as if there was a hidden secret the administrator was trying to uncover. In my heart, the worst fear I had was that Heather's behavior was my fault. And the more I was questioned, the more I feared the administrator would uncover something, whatever that might be, that would place the blame squarely on me.

Once the admission process was finished, I picked up my purse and stood to leave. Without thinking, I called out, "Heather, time to go." A cold chill ran through me as I remembered I was going home without my daughter. Emily offered to take me home, but I declined. I called Steve to pick me up. I asked the administrator if I could say good-bye to Heather and was denied.

As the tears welled up in my eyes, I struggled not to break down right there. Emily walked out with me. I tried walking a few steps ahead of her so she could not see my face, but I know she could sense my pain. When we got to the parking lot, Emily put her arm around my shoulder and asked, "Will you be OK?"

I nodded. I knew if I tried to speak, my cries would spill out of me. After Emily left, I sat alone on the bench, my thoughts racing. I noticed a mother and daughter across the street, holding hands. Suddenly the anguish I felt came rushing out. I doubled over, cupped my hands over my mouth, and wailed like a wounded animal. I became conscious of the noise and attention I was creating, but I could not stop. I cried until I was spent. When I was finally able to stop crying, I quietly waited for Steve to take me home—to my boys.

Once I got home, the routine of preparing dinner and helping the boys with their homework kept my mind busy. But bedtime was excruciating. I tossed and turned all night, replaying the day's events over and over in my mind. I knew my family could not continue living in fear of what Heather might do to herself or someone else and that she would be safe until we could get the answers we needed about her extreme behavior. But that did not take away the pain and guilt of having Heather in an institution.

As I relived the memories of the years leading up to the day's event, I asked myself, *My God, how did we get here?*

June 6, 2001

I'm afraid. Sometimes the fear is so over-whelming I feel like I'm suffocating. I'm afraid we will never find an answer to what is tormenting Heather. I'm afraid I did something wrong to mess up my kid. I'm so tired of being afraid, I just want it to go away.

Part Two:
Heather, the Early Years

My Beautiful Baby Girl

Heather, the second of my three children, was born in September 1985. My pregnancy and her delivery were very easy. After delivery, I anxiously held out my arms to hold her. This sense of urgency was heightened because of the circumstances of Michael's birth.

Michael, my oldest child, was born in August 1982, with an opening in his stomach and the intestines outside his body. There was no time for me to hold him, even for a minute, as he was immediately whisked away to surgery.

As Heather was placed in my arms, I took in every feature of her tiny face. I can vividly remember her bright red cheeks, which prompted a friend of mine to nickname her "Rosebud." I pushed the curls on her forehead back and traced her brows with my fingertips. As I stroked her cheek, she squirmed in my arms and opened her eyes slightly. I lay comfortably with her in my arms, caressing her cheeks. I soon learned she really liked having her cheeks caressed—it soothed her.

After a few minutes, a nurse took Heather to the nursery and another took me to my room to rest. I had slept for only two hours when a nurse came to my room to tell me that Heather was put in the infant incubator because her breathing was irregular. The nurse said the doctor did not suspect anything serious and that it was just a precaution. Heather was monitored closely over the next three days, and on the fourth day we went home.

Heather slept uninterrupted each night for about six hours. I put her to bed at 10 p.m., and she usually slept until 4 a.m. Since I was nursing, I always got up with her and sat in the rocker in the living room. One morning, when Heather was about two weeks old, she nursed for a long time. When she finished, she fell asleep. I, too, fell asleep with her in my arms.

When I awoke, Heather was blue around the nose and lips, and her complexion was gray. I gently shook her, but she did not respond. I called out to her. After what seemed like an eternity, she began squirming in my arms. Her color started to turn to a healthier pink. I quickly grabbed my bag and took Heather to the hospital.

Heather's pulse, heart rate, and respiration were monitored. After a few hours, she stopped breathing again. The doctors ordered Heather to be transferred to Loma Linda University Medical Center, in San Bernardino, California, for more extensive testing. Loma Linda is famous for its successful infant heart transplants.

At Loma Linda, Heather was diagnosed with sleep apnea, a disorder in which breathing stops during sleep. As a precaution, she had to wear an apnea monitor. If she stopped breathing, an alarm went off. Many times the noise of the alarm was enough to awaken Heather's immature system and restart her breathing. If that did not work, we had to initiate a series of steps. First, Steve or I gently called her name. If that did not work, we had to gently shake her. If that still did not work, we ran our fingernail sharply across the bottom of her foot. The doctor told us babies hate that. If we still did not get a response, we were told to call 911 and initiate CPR.

For the next four months, the monitor went off anywhere from five to seven times a night. At six months, Heather began experiencing fewer episodes of apnea. By nine months she was free of the monitor.

Later, when Heather was about five years old, a friend of mine lost her baby to SIDS (Sudden Infant Death Syndrome). It was at times like those that I realized how close we came to losing Heather. If I had not awakened with her that night in the rocking chair, Heather might have been another SIDS statistic.

Heather's development amazed me. She was potty-trained

by nine months and talking in nearly complete sentences at thirteen months. I remember remarking to my friends many times about Heather's intellect. There were many times I thought she was a gifted child.

In the fall of 1986, Steve and I decided to take a trip to Iowa to visit his aging grandmother. She had just turned one hundred years old and was, understandably, not doing well. We knew if we didn't visit her quickly, we might not have another chance. The trip was long—three days each way in the car with two young children. Michael was four and Heather was one. Heather and Michael were pals the entire trip and comforted each other in a loving way that siblings do before they reach the age of bickering. During one long stretch, the kids became playful and their laughter infectious.

I turned to look at the backseat and said to Michael, "Michael, I love you." Then I turned to Heather and said, "Heather, I love you!" She gleefully squirmed in her seat and replied, "Mommy, I love you." Her response surprised me. This was the first time she had said the entire sentence. It was such a special moment.

I replied to her, "I love you, too, Heather." Spurred by her new discovery, Heather turned to Steve and said, "Daddy, I love you."

Steve replied, "I love you, too, Heather."

Then she turned to Michael and said, "Mikey, I love you." Before long Heather turned this "I love you" banter into a game. Whenever it got quiet in the car, Heather would start the game with an, "I love you, Mommy." And if I did not respond quickly enough with an "I love you, too, Heather," she would repeat it until I did. Heather did not stop until she included everyone in the car. This game lasted the entire trip. We must have exchanged "I love yous" a hundred times. It gave an otherwise long trip a special touch and a memory I cherish.

When Heather was sixteen months old, I learned that I was pregnant with Mark, our youngest. I was given a prescription of vitamin and iron pills to take daily. With the size of our family growing, Steve and I decided to buy a house. Five days after our decision, we hired a teenage neighbor girl to babysit Heather and Michael while we looked at houses for the afternoon.

When we got home, I immediately began preparing dinner. While it was cooking, I checked in on Heather. She was very still in the crib. Her body sagged in my arms as I picked her up. Afraid she had quit breathing, I put my face up to her nostrils. I got a strong smell of iron from her breath. Instinctively, I checked the medicine cabinet. The lid to my iron pills was open and there were only ten pills left of the three-month supply!

Steve called 911. As I held Heather, I noticed her breathing was very shallow. By the time the ambulance reached the emergency room, Heather's condition was very critical. God was definitely watching over us because a full pediatric trauma team of doctors and nurses from Loma Linda was in the emergency room treating another young child. When they saw the severity of Heather's condition, they began treating her immediately. X-rays of Heather's stomach revealed literally dozens of undigested pills. Pumping Heather's stomach would stop any more iron from being absorbed into her system. It did nothing, however, to fix the damage that had already been done. An overdose of iron is very damaging to the heart.

My sister, Nancy, arrived in the emergency room a few minutes later. Just then the doctor told us that the hospital was not equipped to handle Heather's severe needs, so she was going to be transported to Loma Linda once she was stabilized. After about two hours, the doctors felt Heather was stable enough to transport her. I wanted to ride with her in the ambulance, but I was not allowed. Steve went in one vehicle, and I rode with Nancy. Nancy and I followed closely behind the ambulance. At one point, the ambulance stopped for about ten minutes. Because the paramedics gave me strict orders to stay clear of the ambulance, I could do nothing but sit and wait. It was excruciating not knowing what they were doing and how Heather was. It was not until later that night that I learned that Heather had gone into cardiac arrest.

When we reached Loma Linda, Heather was taken out of the ambulance and wheeled into the emergency room. She was so small strapped down on the gurney. I looked to her, and when our eyes met she quickly turned away. I was overwhelmed with anger, guilt, and sadness for my little girl.

Around midnight, Heather was taken to her room in the intensive care unit. Steve and I met with the doctor. He told us he was concerned about Heather's prognosis over the next few days. He expressed concern about the damage to Heather's heart due to the large quantity of iron she had ingested. Then he said he was even more concerned about Heather's mental health. He said Heather would not respond to the doctors or nurses. She simply lay still in bed, curled up like a ball, and would not make eye contact with anyone. He described the fight-or-flight response in humans and said he thought Heather was not fighting for her life but was giving up.

The nurses set up a cot for me in Heather's room, but I did not use it. Instead I climbed into bed with her and held her. I gently rubbed her cheeks and quietly talked to her. She just lay there with her body curled up tightly, motionless and unresponsive. As I lay with her, I wept quietly. Soon my tears turned to prayers as I asked God, *Please help my baby!*

My faith in God is a very large part of who I am. For as long as I can remember, God's presence has been in my life. My father was in the navy, and my family lived on the military base. I went to church, even as a young child, but not with my family. My parents did not attend church. God was not really talked about in our home. Not that my parents were atheists—they just did not go to church or believe in openly discussing their religious beliefs. Yet at a very young age, I yearned to go to church and hear about this God that a lot of our military neighbors talked about—especially Mrs. Monteza, the elderly lady next door.

Mrs. Monteza's husband had been in the military for more than twenty years and was close to retiring, but he still traveled a lot. Their children were grown and out of the house, but Mrs. Monteza always had a houseful of kids. I spent a lot of time with her, learning how to cook her famous homemade ravioli. At age seven, when I noticed Mrs. Monteza heading to church one Sunday morning, I boldly asked her, "Can I go to church with you?"

Surprised, she grinned and said, "Sure, you can come with me, but you have to ask your mama first."

I quickly ran off to ask my mother and, with her permission, began going to the Southern Baptist church every Sunday with Mrs. Monteza. I enjoyed her company and the energy of the Baptist services and continued going to church with her until my family moved away. The minute my family settled in the new base, I scouted the neighbors to find out who went to church. In no time I found a family willing to let me tag along. This time I went to the local Methodist church. By the time my father retired from the military, just before I entered high school, I must have attended every Christian denomination—from Baptist to Methodist, Catholic, Lutheran, and Presbyterian, interdenominational and nondenominational. Although I chose the Catholic faith as an adult, each denomination gave me a different religious and spiritual experience. I use aspects of each today in my faith and walk with God. As the fear and uncertainty of Heather's outlook consumed my thoughts, I turned to that faith to guide me.

The next day Heather was a little more alert. She still would not reach out to me, but when I looked her way, she held my gaze for a few seconds. Her condition improved each day. By the sixth day, she was released from the hospital. For the next week she was still mostly quiet and introverted. After a month she was more animated and energetic, but she was still aloof. I felt like she was angry with me about her ordeal.

March 23, 1987

I feel Heather pulling away from me. It's not overly obvious; it's the little things. Maybe I'm just being paranoid but she doesn't come to me anymore for hugs and kisses. I have to approach her. When I put her on my lap she quickly gives me a hug, as if to placate me, and then squirms to be let free. I tried to play our "I love you" game yesterday but she just looked at me without responding.

A Strange Change in Behavior

Within three months of Heather's overdose, I noticed a significant change in her behavior. Where she was once quiet, fun-loving, and easygoing, she frequently became anxious, combative, defiant, and hard to please.

I can't say how much of Heather's early childhood behavior was associated with her illness, but looking back, I realize the volatile mood swings she experienced shortly after her overdose were defining moments that began the pattern of behavior anomalies that is associated with bipolar. I have often asked myself if the onset of Heather's mental illness could be attributed to that traumatic experience.

My first clue to Heather's extreme behavior occurred when she was nineteen months old. Heather seemed to reach the terrible twos then. She was beginning to show a strong personality. She told me no a little too loudly and waved her arms a little too forcefully when I denied her requests. If she did not like her food, she would hurl her dishes across the room with as much force as she could muster.

Although she once slept soundly through the night, she began to require very little sleep and was constantly on the go. When she did sleep, she literally crashed on the spot. One time she fell asleep in a semi-standing position. As her need for sleep became less and less, the nightly bedtime routine became an ordeal. This was when I first suspected that the extreme nature of Heather's defiance exceeded the boundaries of "normal" child development.

One night, immediately after I laid her down, she stood in her crib and announced, "No, Mommy . . . I don't want to go night-time!" I gave her another kiss and laid her back down. She sprang back up and started climbing the railing of the crib. It took her just a few minutes to master the climb. Once she reached the top of the rail, she clumsily threw herself out of the crib.

The hard landing startled her, but only for a moment. I picked her up and placed her back in her crib. As soon as I put her back, she jumped out again. I put her in bed for the third time, and again she jumped out of the crib. Landing on the floor, she looked up at me as if to say, "I do not want to go to bed now, and I'm not going to." In disbelief and frustration, I gave up and let her fall asleep on the floor.

Over the next five days, Heather continued to defy me when it came time for her to go to bed. The firmer I was with her, the greater her defiance grew. Steve worked from 4 p.m. to midnight, so he had not witnessed Heather's defiance, and until now I had not said anything to him because I felt foolish that a nineteen-month-old child had the best of me. But when one of Heather's somersaults out of the crib resulted in a black eye, I asked him to come home during Heather's bedtime. I think at first he thought I was exaggerating the situation, but he quickly changed his mind when he witnessed her defiance.

At Heather's age, Steve's stern, manly voice commanded enough respect that she would obey him. However, this was only good for as long as Steve's dinner hour lasted. The minute Steve went back to work around 9 p.m., Heather would get out of the crib. Nothing I said or did deterred her. I quietly gave up. Heather seemed to have won the battle. I questioned my parenting skills and felt frustrated that a toddler had beaten me into submission.

The crib battle lasted for about three months and was resolved when we replaced Heather's crib with a bed. Then the challenge became getting her to stay in her room at night rather than roaming the house. With her need for little sleep, she would be up until the early-morning hours. Her unlimited energy was playing havoc with my sleep. It seemed I just hit the pillow with three or four hours of sleep when Heather would come to the side of my bed in the early-morning hours asking, "Mommy, are you awake?"

Although Heather's behavior confused me, I passed it off as a phase. Her intelligence and willingness to stand up for herself were difficult, but at times admirable. I reasoned that this trait would be of great use later in life, so I should accept the gift of her inner strength and cherish it rather than question it. Eventually I was, at times, able to convince myself that I was overreacting. But a nagging suspicion at the back of my mind would not go away—no matter how hard I tried to ignore it.

May 21, 1987

Heather is such a handful. There are some days I don't know whether to hug her or to spank her. She amazes me with her intelligence and baffles me with her persistence. The situation with her bedtime really confuses me. I don't know whether to let it pass or be concerned. This is a lot harder than I ever imagined.

Continuing Oddities

The mid-to-latter part of 1987 was an exciting time. In August of that year, Michael was five, and I was sending him off to school. That same October, Mark was born. In addition to raising a family, I was attending college part-time for my bachelor's degree in business administration, with a major in accounting and a minor in computer science. As a mother of young children, I often found myself looking back to my childhood to reflect upon the happy moments.

Growing up on a military base was a fascinating experience for me. There was such a sense of community. Neighbors learned to rely on one another, as there were always a couple of military wives in the neighborhood who were alone while their husbands were away at sea—my mother usually being one of them.

My father, an engineman on the navy minesweepers, was away at sea more then he was home. When my father was gone, many other families pitched in to help my mom with household repairs when needed. I had a sense of belonging to many families. I was welcome to walk into most of my neighbors' homes without knocking, as if I were one of their own.

This childhood experience gave me such a wonderful sense of community and family that I knew at a young age that I wanted to have a family of my own. So as my family grew, I was happy being a mother of three young children. Things were as I imagined them. I had the family I always wanted, and I was committed to this being the perfect family.

I finished my degree in December 1988. Graduation did not take place until the spring of 1989. I contemplated whether I was going to attend the ceremonies but in the end decided to go. I am glad I did. The ceremonies were held outdoors, and the day was beautiful and sunny. Steve brought Michael and Heather, but Mark was too young to attend, so he stayed with the babysitter. The size of my graduating class exceeded one thousand, so I stood in line for more than an hour to receive my diploma, but the time passed quickly.

To this day I remember when my name was called to receive my diploma. Just as I climbed the steps to the stage, I heard two children in the audience yell, "Mom, Mom!" I looked back and spotted Michael on his father's shoulders, his legs dangling. Steve held on to Michael's legs with one arm and the other arm cradled Heather. Both kids waved their hands high in the air in the hopes that I would spot them. I found them in the audience and waved back just when the photographer snapped my picture. It was a happy moment that still lives vividly in my memory.

June 24, 1989

Today was such a beautiful day. The weather was perfect for the outdoor ceremonies and it was wonderful to have Steve and Michael and Heather there. Now that I have gradu-ated, I know everything will be fine. I'm sure my struggle with Heather's problems were because of the stress of school. Now I can really focus more on my family. Everything will be fine.

My sister, Nancy, had always watched my kids when needed, but shortly after I graduated, she took a part-time job and could no longer watch them. I had started a job as a programmer, and with Steve working the day shift, I had to find day care for Heather and Mark. I put Heather, three years old, and Mark, one, into the base day care.

Steve had joined the air force just six months after we were married; as a result, we lived on a military base. Having grown up myself on a military base, I felt very comfortable putting my children in the base day care. The military day care is excellent, and the exposure my children got to other people from all races and walks of life was an enriching experience.

At first, Heather played with the kids in the typical fashion that kids play, but within six months she began bullying the other children. She easily resorted to yelling or screaming if the other kids would not give her the toy that she wanted. If this did not scare them into submission, she grabbed the toys out of their hands or stood in the corner of a room with her fist raised at them.

When the adults disciplined Heather, she boldly stared at them in defiance, yelled obscenities, or pointed her finger in their faces and demanded, "Get out of here!" This went on for several months while the day care supervisors tried every means to effectively channel Heather's energy. Their methods met with no success. One day Heather pushed a younger child's face into the toilet. As a result, I was told Heather could no longer come to the day care.

I could not believe that Heather would behave like that. Surely, the day care workers were wrong! I could not imagine how Heather could possibly know this kind of behavior; she certainly did not see it or hear that language in our home. I struggled to come to grips with the fact that Heather was capable of the kind of behavior that prompted her expulsion from day care at the age of four!

I didn't know what to do. My job allowed me to work at home most of the time, but I still had to go into the office to meet with clients periodically. I needed someone to watch the kids for a few hours each day.

I interviewed several women before I selected a day care provider. The woman I hired seemed to have a no-nonsense way of working with children, utilizing a combination of compassion and firmness when discipline was needed. I told her of the incident at the previous day care and she seemed sure things would be fine. Much to my relief, by the end of the first few weeks there were no problems. But the stability lasted for only a short time.

Within a month, Heather started antagonizing the children when she could not get her way. I know children have spats with one another, but Heather's behavior went beyond the normal bounds of child defiance. It appeared that Heather escalated her behavior as the need required it. This usually resulted in the other children giving into Heather's demand out of fear or shock at her behavior. When we tried to correct Heather, she had no regard for the consequences.

Heather's behavior was so confusing to me. I could not understand why a child from a loving, disciplined, Christian home would act out in such a way. Steve and I were doing all the "right things" as parents, so I couldn't understand the reason for Heather's extreme volatility.

As her behavior worsened at the day care, she also showed more problems at home. She began to exhibit on-again, off-again cycles that ranged from extreme sadness to extreme fits of anger and energy. At home or at the day care, Heather was constantly picking fights with the other children—with little or no apparent reason. She impulsively lashed out at anyone. I knew her behavior was not maliciously planned. But, of course, that did not make it all right. Heather's behavior meant Steve or I were constantly apologizing to someone or trying to correct her. The more we tried to correct Heather, the stronger her defiance became. Because I was home with Heather most of the time, I experienced her outbursts more often, and disciplining her was becoming much harder.

One day, when I told her to go to her room for refusing to pick up her toys in the living room, she grabbed a toy, threw it at me and then charged me, screaming and pounding her little fists on my stomach. It did not hurt, of course—at least not physically—but I had a sick feeling growing in the pit of my stomach that told me something was horribly wrong.

At first Heather's mistreatment of others was limited to verbal assaults, either yelling or cursing in words that made me cringe. But as time progressed, the behavior escalated to physical threats toward the other kids. She would pinch or hit the children or grab their toys. She could be very loud at times, often making strange and inappropriate noises that were very distracting for everyone around her. After three months of trying to work with Heather, the day care owner told me she could not handle Heather's explosive behavior anymore. She asked that I find someone else to care for my daughter.

I was frustrated and confused. I could not figure out what made Heather behave the way she did. She had twice been kicked out of a day care facility at the age of four. This behavior was just too extreme to be explained away. My nagging fears could not be allayed by Heather's seeming inability to control her anger. She was not an easy child to manage or predict. One minute she was pounding her little fists against my chest out of anger and frustration, the next she was giving me a hug that melted my heart. At a loss as to how to deal with Heather, Steve and I sought professional counseling to try to understand what we were dealing with.

When we called around to the local psychologists to find out who specialized in child behavioral problems, we learned that none of them would see Heather because they felt she was too young. But many said they would speak with us. We selected a psychologist from the local community who came highly recommended from one of Steve's supervisors and scheduled an appointment at the earliest availability, which ended up being six months later as we struggled to get authorization from our insurance.

Our appointment was scheduled for the early afternoon while the kids were still in school. After a brief wait, we were escorted into the stereotypical psychiatric office. A large cozy sofa was arranged in the middle of the room with a chair just a few feet away. The psychologist motioned for us to take a seat at a round table in the corner of the room. After brief introductions, the psychologist asked Steve and me to describe our concerns about Heather's behavior.

I responded, "Heather is extremely bright for her age in the sense that she is very aware of her circumstances. She has a great deal of energy and a strong personality to the point it quickly scares other kids into giving in to her demands. She could be fine one minute, and then suddenly she might have a fit so violent that it leaves me dumbfounded. Once her fit of anger is over, I'm still left with the effects of it, but Heather acts like nothing happened. That makes trying to correct her explosive behavior next to impossible. She can revert from a high level of energy to near lethargy in a period of days or weeks without any warning signs or apparent reason."

I described Heather's expulsion from the past two day care centers. As I continued describing Heather's behavior, the psychologist interrupted me and said, "I'm sure her behavior isn't as bad as you describe."

I did not know how to respond to the comment. Instead I sat there looking at her, wanting to say, "Do you live with my child?" I got the feeling that she was suggesting that Steve and I were overly sensitive parents. To validate my belief, once Steve and I finished speaking, she stood, patted me on the back, and said, "You are worrying too much—everything will be fine. It's just a phase she will outgrow."

I probably expected too much going into this meeting, but I did not think we deserved to be treated like overzealous parents who did not have a clue about their child's behavior.

The feeling in my gut kept telling me something was seriously wrong, but, at the time, it was easier to explain Heather's behavior away as a passing phase. I left the meeting frustrated. We had sought professional assistance. Instead, I felt patronized, more confused, and the hardest thing of all was that I had no idea what to do next. All we could do was hope Heather's extreme, angry, and seemingly uncontrollable outbursts were truly a phase that she would soon outgrow.

March 15, 1990

Steve and I went to see a psychologist today to help us understand the reasons for Heather's behavior. Boy, was that a big mistake. The psychologist didn't come out and say it, but I felt like she thought we were incompetent parents.

I wish this nagging feeling would go away but I can't let it go. Heather's behavior is just so different. She gets mad so easily and takes it out on me most of the time. I want to hold her and cuddle with her but she very rarely lets me. She only lets me be near her on her terms.

Since I was able to work from home most of the time, I rarely needed a baby-sitter, but I still had to come to the office periodically. I arranged my schedule so that I went into the office on Tuesday and Thursday afternoons. I searched to find a day care provider for Heather during those hours. When I felt I was at the end of my rope, a good friend of mine, Joan, who had two children the same ages as Michael and Heather, offered to care for Heather during my work hours. I was very reluctant to leave Heather with Joan. I even considered taking a leave of absence from work, but our financial position did not make that option a viable one. After a long discussion with Joan, we agreed to try it.

I was on pins and needles for the first month, but after a successful start it seemed that Heather was doing well in Joan's care. Much to my delight, within three months Joan did not report any problems. I did not know until many years later that Joan had a lot of problems with Heather. I think Joan felt it was a reflection of her ability. I feel terrible that she did not tell me about her problems until years later, but I can certainly understand her reasoning.

Through the tumultuous eight-year period of struggling with Heather's severe mood swings and defiant behavior before diagnosis, there were many time I felt like an absolute failure as a parent. It is easy to get caught into the trap of thinking bad behavior in your child must mean that you are a bad parent.

Joan cared for Heather for more than a year before Heather started first grade and attended the after-school program. Heather's behavior at home was often a challenge. Steve and I usually had to tell her numerous times to do something before she would comply, yet we began to accept this as a normal part of Heather's personality.

We viewed Heather as a strong-willed child, but at the time, we tried to look at this as a good trait. By the time Heather turned five, in 1990, and began first grade, she had gone a year without any major incidents of her past disruptive behavior. I began to feel that I had been overexaggerating the severity of Heather's past behavior, and that my fears and concerns were unfounded. I thought, perhaps, the psychologist was right and it was a phase that Heather had outgrown.

In the spring of 1991, Steve left the air force. After ten years in the military, it was a big change for our family, but Steve was eager to start a new career. He began working as a software engineer for one of the defense contractors in Los Angeles. His job was interesting, but it meant he had to spend a lot of time on the road. We had bought a house the year before so we had already made the transition off base, which was definitely an adjustment for my family.

With the ninety-minute commute each way, Steve had to leave the house no later than 5:45 a.m., and he usually did not get home until around 7:30 p.m. Steve enjoyed his job, but it didn't take long for this schedule to take a toll on the time we had as a family.

July 23, 1991

Steve is gone so often that I have to be the one to discipline the kids most of the time. He has to work such long hours. Many times he comes home when the kids are in bed.

He comes home from a long day of work and I want to talk with him. But he's often tired and I don't want to burden him. Sometimes I feel like it's just me and the kids and this instinct that something isn't right.

While Heather was in the first and second grades, some of her old ways came out from time to time. She struggled with either highly-energized behavior that resulted in wildly-frenzied outbursts, or depressive lows that left her with little interest in the day-to-day joys of life, but they did not last long. In between, there was a longer calm period, so we dealt with each episode as best we could.

Although each episode sparked a new crisis, Steve and I quickly learned the art of rapid adjustment. During the interval between episodes, my family enjoyed our daily routines and Heather resumed a healthy childhood development. With each episode, I hoped that the last "bad" period was just a passing phase. Each time, I was able to convince myself it was all behind us. Heather spent a lot of her time with our elderly widow neighbor, Gina, visiting for hours—talking, cooking, or helping with the gardening. They enjoyed each other's company. Heather gave Gina a youthful mind that Gina soaked up, and Gina gave Heather unlimited attention.

By the third grade, Heather, almost eight, took a turn for the worse. She made impossible demands on everyone in our family and was unhappy with almost anything we tried to do for her.

Her behavior could generally be described as excessive. When she was sad, she would isolate herself in her room for hours on end. Trying to engage her in family activities was difficult at best, and many times impossible. When she did join us during her low times, she would just sit there or even fall asleep. When she was unhappy with her circumstances, she usually responded out of proportion to what one might expect. For example, one evening when Heather was done with her homework, she decided to watch TV. When Heather went downstairs and saw the boys already in front of the television, she immediately ordered them to turn the channel to her favorite program. When they did not respond, she began loudly cursing and pounding her fists against the walls yelling, "Turn the damn TV to my show!"

Rather than accept the fact that she would not get to watch her program, Heather started kicking and banging her fists against the walls and threw the remote and soda bottles across the room. Because Steve was gone, I had to deal with Heather's outburst—a chore I was beginning to dread.

I raced downstairs to see what all the commotion was about. When I came into the room, my presence did not calm Heather; it only fueled her anger. She continued her tirade. As the boys stared at her in stunned disbelief, I stood there yelling, "Heather, stop it!" My demands did not dissuade her as she went on until her energy was spent. Then, all at once, Heather bolted up the stairs. I stepped in front of her, trying to get her to speak to me. Instead she pushed me aside without saying a word, giving me a look that said, "What are you looking at?" I stood there thinking, *This is not normal behavior. Doesn't she understand that?*

I followed her upstairs to her bedroom and tried to talk with her, but she slammed the door in my face, barricading herself in her bedroom for the rest of the night. When Steve came home, we talked about the incident but neither of us really had an answer. We were truly beginning to realize just how little control we had over Heather's behavior. When her moods got out of whack, she did not respond to any discipline Steve and I provided.

I worried the entire evening, trying to understand what was raging inside Heather to make her so unhappy and volatile for no apparent reason. It was even more frustrating because she would not let me get close enough to help her.

Heather's behavior was having a huge impact on her brothers. She knew exactly how to annoy them, and there were many fights that resulted in Steve or me having to intervene because Heather got too physical with them. And she was getting into trouble at school so often that she was suspended five times within the first half of third grade. Steve and I began to see a disturbing pattern of behavior with Heather: A pattern in which each new cycle of explosive behavior escalated in severity, increasing frequency, and duration. As the pattern continued, Steve and I began to fear that we were not just dealing with a strong-willed child, but with something much more serious, something that was not going to go away on its own.

With each school suspension, Steve and I tried to get the school principal and counselors to see that Heather's episodes were not isolated but a part of a larger pattern of behavior that needed to be treated as a whole.

We hoped that if the school counselors could see this behavior holistically, they could see that Heather needed help and not merely punishment. But since Steve and I are not mental-health professionals, we did not really know how to impress upon them our concerns. Instead, each incident resulted in Heather missing more and more school and the administrator's continued advice to us that we take parenting classes.

During the latter part of the third grade, Heather became explosive on the school bus and punched a boy in the stomach. This, of course, brought another school suspension. This time the suspension was not the usual five days, it was for three weeks! Fortunately, I had the kind of job that I could do from home. I dealt with Heather's suspensions by working with her at home to complete her homework assignments and keep her studies up to date.

Heather did not have many childhood friends. She seemed to be more comfortable with older kids or adults. She had an intelligence and an uncanny ability to perceive and manipulate things around her that turned off the other kids her age. Steve and I realized that Heather understood adult conversations and issues at a young age, so we had to watch what we said around her.

Because we lived in southern California, we experienced our share of earthquakes. In the spring of 1993, there were two fairly large earthquakes, called the twin quakes in Yucca Loma. Seven-year-old Heather's experience during these earthquakes left her with an extreme fear of them. Through my childhood years living in southern California, I had never experienced earthquakes of those magnitudes. So the twin quakes were scary for me, too.

At 3:30 a.m. on January 17, 1994, Heather came to the side of my bed and awakened me. With a trembling voice she asked, "Mommy, can I sleep with you?"

I asked, "What's wrong?"

Heather said, "I'm scared we're going to have an earthquake."

I did not take her seriously, but I let her sleep with me. I curled up next to her and, in little time, we both fell soundly back to sleep. Within thirty minutes, we were awakened by the violent shaking of the bed. As my senses became more alert, I realized we were in the middle of a major earthquake. Items were falling off the bathroom shelf and several pictures fell off the walls in the living room, crashing to the ground. The intensity of the quake made me think this was the "big one." Suddenly, the house jolted. I could see the big chandelier in the hallway swaying back and forth, nearly crashing into the ceiling.

When the first jolt hit, Heather jumped out of bed and said, "I knew it, I knew we were going to have an earthquake!"

Seismologists later said the quake lasted no more than one minute, but it felt like an eternity. During the shaking, many thoughts went through my mind. I was amazed at Heather's composure, instead of fear, during the shaking. It seemed that her perceived foreknowledge of the event took away her fears, as if she now had command of the situation.

Steve was already on his way to work, and Michael and Mark were spending the night with friends. Steve worked in Pico Rivera, just miles from the epicenter in Northridge, California. Immediately after the quake, the phone lines were dead. This heightened my uncertainty because I had no way of knowing for several hours how Steve and the boys fared. Within a few minutes the trembling ceased, and Heather, looking up at me, said, "Oh boy, that was bad!"

I responded, "Yes it was. Now Mommy has to go check the house to make sure everything is okay."

I put her back in bed while I checked around, and fortunately nothing structurally was damaged, and we still had water, gas, and electricity. In the end, we fared well; my family was unharmed, and there was no damage to our home. This was great news because Steve and I had already made plans to leave southern California, but first we had to sell our house.

Part Three:

Journey into the Darkness of the Unknown

The Move to the Midwest

Steve and I were growing increasingly tired of southern California and were eager to move to the Midwest, where the majority of our family lived. Just two weeks after the earthquake, we made separate trips to the Midwest for job interviews. The trips were successful. We each received great offers to start new jobs in Omaha, Nebraska, as soon as possible. We had two months to sell our home, pack up our belongings, and relocate from sunny southern California to the vast openness of the Midwest.

It was a hectic time, but our family was full of anticipation. We longed to be closer to our extended family and to be in a part of the country that had more to offer by way of scenery, wide-open spaces, and great job opportunities.

I came out first to find a house to rent and start my job. Steve and the kids stayed in California another month to complete the sale of the house and to finish last-minute business.

We timed the move so that Steve and the kids would travel the weekend before Easter break. They arrived Tuesday morning of spring break, much to the chagrin of the kids, who missed no school because of the move. Our first Sunday together in our new home was Easter Sunday. At the time, I thought the day had great significance—a new beginning. I hoped it would be a new start for Heather—a fresh slate to begin a new school and find new friends.

Steve and the kids used the rest of the week to recuperate from the trip and enroll in their schools. Because my father was transferred a lot in the navy, I moved around a lot, so I knew firsthand the traumatic experience of a move. Steve and I tried to make the transition as easy as possible for the kids. We found a nice house in an established neighborhood. There were plenty of children for our kids to play with. The elementary school was just one block from our home, and the middle school, which Michael would attend, was fewer than three blocks away.

The next week the kids started school, and Steve started his job. He had a contract for consulting work at the air force base and worked the second shift, 4 p.m. to midnight, training military personnel. Steve and I always tried to stagger our work schedule when the kids were young to minimize the amount of time they spent in day care, so it was good to have Steve back on this schedule. Steve saw the kids off to school in the morning and left for work just as Michael arrived home after school. I spent the evening with the kids.

The first few days in their new schools seemed OK as the kids adjusted to their teachers and classmates. But by Friday of the first week, Heather's elementary school principal called me. He said the teacher was having problems with Heather's classroom behavior and that Heather seemed tense, frequently yelling at the teacher or other students. He asked me if Heather angered easily. A sense of panic crept into me.

To mask my concern, I tried to act calm and convince myself that Heather's behavior was a result of her anxieties about the move. I silently reasoned that the objectionable behavior would go away after another week. I tried to sound convincing as I assured the principal—and myself—that Heather was probably upset with the transition to the new environment. I suggested that the stress of having to meet so many new children was temporary. I asked him to be patient.

He said, "I understand how difficult this must be for Heather." He assured me that he and the teachers would help her with the transition. I hung up the phone and sat in a daze for a few minutes. My thoughts raced in fear and denial. I had hoped the move would provide a fresh start for Heather. I naively thought it would wipe away all her past behaviors. The phone call created doubt.

From that point on, the circumstances at school only worsened. The principal called again the next week. This time Heather got in a fight with a boy in her classroom. She was given an in-school suspension, her first one in the second week of a new school. In no time, Heather's combative behavior frightened the other children. As a result, none of them would play with her. Heather was often confused by her behavior; many times she cried out to me that she could not understand why she acted the way she did and promised that she would change. She was mostly alienated and left alone to deal with the confusing emotions raging inside her. It broke my heart to see Heather so isolated. Yet every time she befriended someone, the relationship did not last long because her behavior scared the kids away.

Because we moved in the latter part of the school year, the kids had only two and a half months left before summer break. By the end of the first month, it seemed that Heather spent more time out of school then in. It was a tumultuous time. Steve and I were adjusting to new jobs and trying to help the kids adjust to the new environment. Dealing with the turmoil as a result of a move was tiring enough, but dealing with the emotional and logistical issues as a result of Heather's behavior was exhausting. So, for a long time, I did not tell our family or friends of our circumstances. Many times I felt so alone.

During the remainder of the school year, Heather's behavior continued to escalate. One day in early May, the principal called me. He explained that Heather became combative with the teacher and was sent to the principal's office. Heather refused to go to the principal's office, and instead climbed the bookshelf in the hall. Once on the bookshelf, which was about ten feet in the air, she threatened to jump. Fortunately, the school staff was able to bring her down safely.

Steve and I were at our wits' end. Heather was constantly ignoring the school rules and disrupting the classroom, with absolutely no regard for consequences or the safety of herself and others.

As Heather's behavior worsened, Steve and I requested an evaluation by the Student Assistance Team, a function of special education, to determine if Heather would qualify for special-education services. Steve and I felt we needed help from the school professionals to better understand the reasons for Heather's behavior. We so badly needed to know what we were dealing with. Otherwise, any attempts to alleviate the circumstances were futile. But the school officials thought that Heather's behavioral difficulties were of "insufficient duration" to merit such an evaluation.

I did not exactly know what the results would provide, but I felt that trying something was better than doing nothing. But the special-education rules were clear and gave no room for flexibility. We continued living our lives, day by day, often frustrated and confused by Heather's extreme behavior. During the next few weeks, it became a daily routine to receive a call from Heather's teacher or principal to discuss her behavior.

Heather was so volatile that Steve and I doubted the situation could quickly turn around, so we decided to take her out of school for the final three weeks. I thought the principal would discourage us, but he agreed that in light of the current circumstances it would be best to remove Heather, seek professional help during the summer, and reassess the situation in early fall before the next school year.

Because of our previous experience with the psychologist in California, Steve and I had not yet sought help from another professional. We knew we could not continue dealing with Heather's behavior without the assistance of a child psychologist. Through the recommendation of the school principal, we called Lanette Parker and scheduled an appointment to meet with her as soon as possible.

Initially I dreaded the meeting with Ms. Parker and went into it with a great deal of anxiety. But she made me feel welcome and comfortable. Before long, I found myself opening up to her. During our first session, Ms. Parker talked with Heather briefly and then spent the remainder of the time with Steve and me, getting background information. Midway through our session, Ms. Parker asked us to share our concerns and observations regarding Heather's behavior. I answered, "I'm afraid she has bipolar disorder." I said this because of my past experience with this behavior from my mother's sister—my aunt Suzie.

I did not know Suzie as I was growing up because I spent most of my early years in southern California, and Suzie and her family lived in the Midwest. When my father retired from the navy, my family moved back to the Midwest. I was in high school when I met Suzie, and, other than at a few family events, I did not really have many interactions with her. When I graduated from high school and went to college for nurses' training, Suzie was also in nurses' training. She went back to school after her children were grown. Since we were in the same classes, we got to know each other better. Suzie was a very good student, and I even relied on her for help sometimes. Then suddenly, toward the middle of the semester, Suzie's behavior changed, and she was cranky and surly most of the time.

At first Suzie took her irritable moods out on everyone. After I approached her one afternoon and asked her if she was OK, she turned her anger toward me. Soon it was unbearable to be around her. She often yelled at me for no reason. One day she even publicly accused me of trying to make her fail.

I was embarrassed and confused by her behavior, so one day I asked my mother about Suzie. My mother told me that my aunt had always had problems as a child, but her problems really got bad when she was in her late twenties—so bad that Suzie had to be placed in a state mental-health institution for more than a year until she was properly diagnosed and treated for bipolar. I recall my mother saying to me, "Leslie, you ought to know that bipolar runs in families." At the time, this situation was all very interesting but really did not mean much to me.

Dealing with Heather's behavior, I had an eerie sense of déjà vu related to the Suzie's behavior and began to worry that Heather might have inherited this illness.

Ms. Parker listened to my suggestion and said, "I can't make a diagnosis yet, but I know doctors are finding that child-onset mental illness will usually manifest itself fully between seven and eleven years of age." Well, Heather was eight at the time, and whatever was the cause for her behavior was manifesting itself now!

I also expressed concern to Ms. Parker that the trauma of the move may have triggered something in Heather, making her explosive behavior more volatile. Ms. Parker, sensing my concern, said,

"Although the move may have been highly stressful, if this really is a mental illness, such as bipolar, anything else could have been a triggering event. It would have just been a matter of time before something set it off."

Although my fears were difficult for me to put in words, voicing them elicited a mixture of relief and guilt. I had held in my fears for so long that to finally express them was a relief. At the same time, I so wanted to be wrong.

We continued the therapy sessions with Ms. Parker, and after several months and further testing, Ms. Parker concluded that Heather suffered with impulse-control disorder.

Perhaps this described Heather's incident at school one day. The principal called to tell me that Heather had stolen her class's fund-raising money. I was humiliated, and my face burned with anger. The principal said that when Heather was confronted, she readily admitted the theft and returned the money. I could not understand why Heather would do this. She later told me, "I probably shouldn't have taken the money," and tried to explain away the theft as a bad mistake. She shrugged and said, "It was something I just did without thinking about it."

This behavior is a classical example of impulsive behaviors that Ms. Parker described. Ms. Parker explained, "The impulsive person suffers with persistent ideas, images, or impulsive actions that are not logical or rational. As a result, Heather does, says, or acts upon whatever comes to mind." This incident, once again, broadened the boundaries of Heather's behaviors.

Ms. Parker described Heather as having an impaired social life and impulsive affect. Even though the professionals gave a fancy medical description for Heather's behavior, it did nothing to improve the circumstances.

May 12, 1994

We met with another therapist today and she was much better than the last one. I felt comfortable enough that I finally opened up and shared with her my suspicion that Heather may have bipolar. Putting voice to my fears surprised me. The second the words were out of my mouth I wanted to take them back. I see the same behavior in Heather that I saw in Suzie. God, don't let this be the cause of my little girl's suffering.

Early in the summer, my sister-in-law, Brenda, and her two children planned to visit her sister, Katy (my other sister-in-law), who lived on a farm in a neighboring state. Brenda invited my kids along. Because my kids had only lived in the big city, they looked forward to visiting a farm.

I offered our van to Brenda since she would be traveling with five children. She accepted and packed up our van, heading for a six-hour drive with five children for a three-week stay at Katy's. Up until then, no one outside of my immediate family had spent much time with Heather, so I tried to prepare Brenda for the behaviors she might encounter. After I described Heather's past behavior, Brenda said it did not concern her enough to exclude Heather. I said a prayer that the trip would go smoothly for everyone, especially Heather.

Much to my disappointment, it did not. Evidently, Heather became argumentative and defiant not long after they departed. Her behavior only escalated from there. I called periodically to speak with the kids during the visit, but I did not get a sense from either of my sisters-in-law of the difficulty they were having with Heather until the third week. Katy told me that Heather frequently yelled at others and became easily agitated for no apparent reason. I felt helpless to do anything because they were six hours away, and any advice I gave them was met with the response, "We tried that."

Upon returning home, Brenda explained the problems she had with Heather. The more Brenda described the events of the trip, the worse I felt for her and my family. I could imagine all too well the frustration they went through while trying to deal with Heather's combative behavior. This trip only increased our concern about the frequency and severity of Heather's extreme, disruptive acts.

For the rest of the summer, Steve and I tried to minimize the potential for explosive behavior from Heather by keeping a close and watchful eye on her. Desperate measures called for creative ideas, and Steve and I were learning to be very creative.

Fortunately, the summer went by with relative calm. Heather still had problems periodically but the manic episodes were less volatile, with longer intervals of calm in between. Because Steve was home most of the day during the week, he and the kids spent much of their time taking trips to the fishing pond. During the evenings, the kids and I spent many warm nights at Dairy Queen, trying out the newest sensations. And on weekends, my family spent most of our time at the swimming pool or taking long drives in the country. The peaceful time was a much-needed break from the turmoil of the past and provided my family with many happy memories to get us through the rough times ahead.

June 24, 1994

I think we should cut back on our visits to the other family members until Heather gets better. Her behavior is very difficult for me to understand. How can I expect them to understand? I really hate to do this, but I don't know what else to do.

Fourth Grade

To prepare for the coming school year, about two weeks before classes were scheduled to begin, Steve and I met with Heather's assigned fourth-grade teacher. We discussed with him the circumstances of Heather's behavior and tried to identify a plan to prevent her potential outbursts—and if that failed, to positively manage her behavior in the event she became combative. We described Heather's behavior pattern in order to prepare him for what he might encounter. He listened intently to our concerns, and then assured us that he would work with Heather to provide a successful school year. Although we were very hopeful this teacher would be successful, we were also wary.

Heather's problematic behavior began almost immediately. Her behavior grew to include spontaneous noises, whistling and singing, daydreaming, arguing, destruction of property, and lack of cooperation with the school staff. Within a short time, Heather increasingly had problems with her peers. She frequently yelled, screamed, jabbed others with pencils, and elbowed and fought with many of her schoolmates.

By December 1994, the situation was not getting any better. Steve and I made another request for a special-education evaluation. This time it was granted.

The evaluation was meant primarily to determine Heather's general level of intellectual and behavioral development. Problems in intellectual development can sometimes result in irritable behavior because of a child's frustration in trying to accomplish tasks that are beyond her ability.

Problems with behavioral development can exhibit themselves when a child's social maturity is not even with peers of her age. If this is the case, the child feels a great deal of stress and conflict, causing her to lash out to others.

The information would help determine if Heather's behavior was a result of developmental problems, a learning disorder, or something else. I wanted to make sure we could help Heather by treating the cause of her problems and not merely putting a Band-Aid on the symptoms.

The findings of the evaluation were interesting. Heather's intellectual level was rated average to above average, and she, when keeping up with her work, performed at or above grade level. But the behavioral assessment placed Heather within range of significance for anxious and aggressive behaviors (depression, social problems, thought problems).

As described by her teacher, "Heather demonstrates dramatic mood swings and frequently loses control of her temper." Specific behaviors of concern cited by the teacher included humming or making other odd noises in class; inappropriately expressing emotions relative to the situation (for example, she laughed at a grieving student whose grandmother had just died); arguing; defiance; destroying property; and being uncooperative with classmates.

The psychologist who performed the evaluation stated that "Heather has poor ability for a child her age to identify and solve interpersonal problems." He further noted that "she tended to verbalize superficial and unrealistic resolutions to problem situations and her responses could often be characterized as maladaptive and tended to reflect anger." For example, if Heather was asked why she hit another child she would say, "He made me angry so I hit him." The most troubling, however, were the ominous drawings of death that Heather presented during one of the evaluations. When talking with the psychologist, Heather expressed extreme sadness and loneliness, and talked in great detail of how she might end her life.

As a result of the assessment, Heather qualified for special-education services in a behaviorally disordered (BD) category. Based on the federal and state regulations, behaviorally disordered means a condition exhibiting one or more of the following characteristics over a long period and to a marked degree, which adversely affect the child's educational performance or, in the case of children below age five, development:

1) An inability to learn that can not be explained by intellectual, sensory, or health factors.
2) An inability to build or maintain satisfactory inter-personal relationships with peers and teachers.
3) Inappropriate types of behaviors or feelings under normal circumstances.
4) A general pervasive mood of unhappiness or depression.
5) A tendency to develop physical symptoms or fears associated with personal or school problems.

Following the evaluation, Steve and I met with the special-education team to develop an Individualized Educational Program (IEP in educator's lingo). Even though Steve and I had asked for the evaluation, we struggled with mixed emotions about Heather being labeled as "behaviorally disordered." But we learned to swallow our pride because we knew we were not equipped to handle Heather's behavior without professional help. We soon learned that we had to develop thick skin when it came to comments by others when they learned that Heather was in special-education for a behavior disor-der.

One day when I was at school picking up my kids, another parent learned that Heather was in the BD class. She approached me and asked, "Don't you know how to discipline your child?"

I wanted to say to her, "How do you discipline a child who would rather hurt herself than listen to your corrections? How do you discipline a child who has no regard for consequences? How do you discipline a child who deals with such painful rage inside that the witnessing of it breaks your heart?" Instead, I simply said, "I hope you never have to deal with this."

Heather's initial IEP established two hours a day of special-education tutoring. The rest of the day she was in the mainstream classroom. After a month in the BD classroom, there seemed to be no improvement in Heather's volatile behavior, so Steve and I asked the school officials to increase Heather's time with the special-education instructor. We hoped additional support would give Heather the kind of environment in which she could thrive. Instead, we were told that Heather was not on her current level long enough to warrant additional support.

Not long after that, Heather had a severe episode in her mainstream classroom where she became unruly and combative. She was given an opportunity to take a time-out, but she refused this chance each time it was offered.

She refused to work or follow instructions. She wandered around the classroom. She left and returned to the classroom three times, each time aimlessly wandering outside of the building. She yelled at the other students and threw or kicked their belongings. She pushed the intercom button to the office, cursing in the microphone. She whistled loudly in the students' ears, played with the lights, and knocked over the desks. Amazingly enough, the principal was not summoned until Heather spat in the teacher's face. The principal called me at work to describe the circumstances. I was flabbergasted by the events and upset that the school officials allowed Heather's behavior to escalate that far.

Heather was suspended from school for three days. The principal described the reasons for Heather's suspension this way: "Heather presents a clear threat to the physical safety of herself or others; she uses violence, force, or threats to interfere with school; she causes, or attempts to cause, damage to school property; and her conduct is so extremely disruptive as to make temporary removal necessary to preserve the rights of other students to pursue an education."

I asked the principal if, when Heather returned to school, she would be placed in a full-time special-education classroom away from the stimulus of the regular classroom. He reminded me that Heather was not on her current level long enough to warrant additional support.

"What does time have to do with it? You just told me she is a clear threat to the physical safety of herself and others."

Steve and I felt that Heather needed to be taught by teachers trained in the special-education field. We were concerned that the school did not appreciate the severity of Heather's escalating behavior and that Heather could not thrive in the mainstream school setting.

Regular teachers, unless they receive additional training for behavior disorders, don't have the knowledge and training to effectively deal with Heather's kind of behavior. In this instance, Heather's behavior escalated to an extreme level before the school took action.

Steve and I felt that Heather needed an environment that would protect her and others when she became out of control, an environment that could provide the relative consequences based on a behavioral-therapy model. Home suspension was a ludicrous consequence for Heather's behavior. It did not enforce the cause-and-effect lesson that is critical to a child's social and behavioral development. Suspensions only gave Heather what she wanted, which, in turn, fed her disregard for consequences.

I asked the principal, "Can't you put her in with a full-time special-education instructor?"

He responded, "Let's give it more time on Level I."

The federal and state special-education program identifies levels of services based on a scale of one to three. The least restrictive, Level I, is an in-school setting. This level is intended to provide as much mainstreaming for the student as her handicap will allow. In a special-education program, students are usually limited in their exposure to like students. This reduces their exposure to things that can provide greater challenges and improve their social and educational development. Without mainstreaming, the special-education student's potential to excel beyond her handicap is lessened.

Level II is still an in-school setting, but it involves more time in the special-education classroom and less time in a mainstreamed environment.

Each in-school level involves a minimum number of hours of support a week with a special-education instructor. Within each level, the goal is to reduce the amount of special education a student receives in order to learn to develop the skills and child development he or she needs to grow into maturity.

Level III is the most restrictive, institution-like setting. Students in this level are considered severe in their need for support services. This level requires trained professionals, and there are no mainstreaming opportunities for the child.

The obligation of a public education system is to place a child in the least restrictive setting possible while still supporting her special needs and providing a free, appropriate education. The federal and state special-education process is a federally mandated and subsidized program. Based on our experience, Steve and I came to view it as a very rigid, bureaucratic process with strict guidelines. We soon found out that identified levels of assistance fall within a range of support services and that any movement in the levels, up or down, can only happen one level at a time—and only after specific criteria have been followed for an established time within each level.

Because Heather was at Level I, the school district had to follow the procedures by the book and could not escalate her to Level II yet. She had to be in Level I for a longer time before a reevaluation would be provided for the next level; this was the reason for their dismissal of our request.

I had so much hope that this move into the special-education process would be the first step to a productive treatment plan for Heather. Instead, it was the first step of a long journey that became an arduous, bureaucratic process of dealing with a school system that was inadequately equipped to understand, let alone deal with, the severity of Heather's behavior.

During Heather's suspensions, she usually completed her work with little prodding from me. But by this time she had little interest in anything. Where she once enjoyed reading or riding her bike, she now engaged in very few, if any, outdoor or extracurricular activities.

Steve and I tried to include her in our outings, but she showed no interest. Dealing with her erratic behavior was such an emotional roller coaster. It clearly robbed Heather and my family of many moments of happiness. By now her demeanor seemed to be either combative or sullen—nothing in between. The moments of happiness between us were becoming rare.

Within two weeks of Heather's return to school, the principal called to tell me to come to the school right away. After a confrontation with one of the other kids, Heather became upset and purposely ran out of the school and into oncoming traffic. Thank God the school staff reached her and brought her back to the school before she injured herself. But once released, she tried to run away again.

It took three teachers to hold her at bay, and the school staff had no choice but to restrain her. When Steve and I got to the school, I was not prepared to see Heather being held to the ground by three large men. Her hands were held behind her back and her face pressed firmly to the floor. Each time one of the teachers lessened his grip on her, Heather would bolt up and he would have to hold her even tighter. All the while, Heather was babbling or screaming incoherently. I got down on the floor with her and tried to calm her down by talking to her, but she only got angrier. So we waited.

As the teachers were holding Heather, Steve and I watched, not knowing what to do. We talked with the principal, stalling for time, in hopes that our appearance of calm would make Heather feel less threatened. About fifteen minutes passed before Heather became more lucid. Then she went into a semicatatonic state, simply staring into space.

Heather would not respond when I called her name. I was confused and very concerned. I suggested to Steve that we take Heather to the hospital. She wasn't bleeding and she didn't have any broken bones or physical injuries to speak of, so I didn't know if she should go to the emergency room. I had no idea how to treat an illness of the mind—I felt so inadequate.

Fortunately Heather began to respond to us, and within another fifteen minutes she regained her composure and we were on our way home, as if nothing had happened. Heather's mood swings were mind-boggling. They could go from highly explosive, energized rage to dangerously quiet, introverted behavior faster than Steve or I could adjust from one to the next. Many times I felt as if I were being hit by a tidal wave. Before I could recover from the first wave, I had no time to brace myself for the next one. With the swing of Heather's mood pendulum, another crisis was averted. The remainder of the day brought a welcome but eerie calm.

During the rest of the school year, Heather was continually fighting with other students and cursing or yelling at her teachers, which, of course, resulted in further suspensions and alienation toward Heather and my family from other classmates and parents. The effects of being shunned by neighbors and friends because of Heather's illness took a big toll on my family.

One Friday in early March 1995, Heather's teacher called and asked me to meet with him. I agreed to see him before I picked up the kids from day care.

The minute I walked into his classroom he said to me, "You and your husband have a very serious problem on your hands. If you don't get professional help for Heather now things will only get worse."

Before he could say anything more, I interrupted him and said, "I know we need help, but we don't know where to find the answers. Heather's behavior has been extreme since she was very little, but we don't know how to find the right place for help."

I had a captive audience and I was going to take advantage of it. "We do not abuse or neglect our children," I said, "I can't understand why Heather acts out this way."

I told him of Heather's history of excessive and aggressive behaviors since the preschool years. I tried to explain that I suspected her problems began as early as nineteen months of age. My chest seemed to shrink as I continued to ramble. I went on and on about my fears and before long I was very agitated.

When I calmed down and stopped talking for a minute he said, "I asked to speak with you because I feel that you and your husband need to be aware of the gravity of the situation. With what you say, it is apparent that you and your husband do not need to be convinced. Too often I have seen other parents who will not accept the reality of their situation, but because you and your husband do, you are many years ahead of the problem."

I finally felt validated!

It meant so much to me at the time to have someone else accept that Heather was not merely a stubborn child acting out for attention or that Steve and I were dimwitted parents.

This was so important because I did not want to hide behind this behavior. Instead, I was on a desperate search for the truth, so we could beat whatever it was causing Heather to act out so aggressively. Naming and owning this thing was the first step toward fighting it. Without that, we could only react to the next crisis with no hope for a productive future.

This meeting gave me an even greater determination to continue seeking answers to the unknown questions of Heather's behavior.

After sharing the teacher's comments with Steve, we discussed the teacher's recommendation and realized that we should consider his advice to seek help from a psychiatrist. Ms. Parker, a psychologist, could treat Heather for intensive therapy and parental counseling, but she was not licensed to prescribe medications. She suggested to Steve and me that we consider medications as an option for Heather's treatment—something only a psychiatrist could prescribe.

Steve and I had been very reluctant to place Heather on medications for fear that a quick-fix attitude would cause the doctors and educators to rely solely on the medications, which might mask the symptoms rather than treat the underlying problem. But as Heather's behaviors became more extreme, we realized we had to try all methods of treatment.

We found a child psychiatrist, Dr. Quinlen, who came highly

recommended from Ms. Parker. After extensive evaluation of Heather, Dr. Quinlen concluded that she was suffering from the affects of Attention Deficit Hyperactivity Disorder (ADHD). He placed Heather on two medications, Ritalin and Clonodine. Ritalin is the common medication for ADHD patients.

ADHD is probably the most well known of the mental-health disorders in children. There are an estimated five million children with ADHD in the United States. Children affected with this disorder suffer with hyperactivity, irritability, and a short attention span. This behavior leads many children to be labeled as troublemakers or bullies. Because of this, many children struggle with the effects of this disorder for years before parents, educators, and doctors finally see that the child's behavior is a result of an illness and not simply a result of bad parenting.

Because this condition frequently is accompanied by some degree of learning disability, ADHD constitutes a major problem for school systems.

Ritalin is actually a stimulant. It seems odd that a child struggling with hyperactivity, distractibility, and a short attention span would be given a stimulant. But in children struggling with ADHD, the stimulant has the opposite affect. It liberates the release of neurotransmitters in the brain and causes an increase in wakefulness, alertness, and attention span.

With most medications for the brain, there is a latency period before the medication becomes effective. An antibiotic, for example, works quickly on controlling an infection, but because psychiatric drugs affect the nervous system, they require a period of readjustment before they can be effective.

The first attempts at medicating Heather were horrible. Within five weeks she lost more than fifteen pounds, and she was more irritable than before. She began to have hallucinations at night.

Around midnight one night, Heather cried out from her bed with a guttural sound like a cry of sheer terror; it gave me chills. I jumped out of bed and went to Heather's side. She was shaking violently, with her eyes wide open, staring at the closet, insisting that someone was in there waiting to kill her. I tried to assure her that she was safe, but she would not be comforted by my words so I lay with her for the rest of the night.

When I called Dr. Quinlen the next day, he decreased the dosage. Within a few days, Heather's side effects lessened but in the long run, the medication did not seem to have any positive effect.

About two weeks later, when Heather was getting undressed to take a bath, I noticed sores all over her right arm—not just one or two sores, but more than twenty, each the size of a dime or larger. When I asked Heather how she got them, she shrugged and did not respond.

The next morning, I called the school and spoke with Heather's teacher, hoping to find out how Heather got the sores. The teacher was not able to tell me either. Unbeknownst to me, Heather had inflicted the sores on herself at home. I learned later, during a session with Dr. Quinlen, that Heather told him she cut up her arm with a sharp object, as Heather stated, "just for the heck of it."

March 24, 1995

Heather has sores all over her arm. I learned today that she did it to herself. It's almost like she is turning her anger inward.

Her First Hospitalization

By April 1995, at age nine, Heather's episodes of aggression were becoming even more frequent and volatile. Her flash point, the time in which her anger turned into uncontrollable rage, lessened with each episode. One minute she could be sitting in class working attentively, and the next minute, for no apparent reason, she would react violently to something. Eventually her extreme behavior resulted in the first of many in-patient hospitalizations.

In early April, Steve and I were getting ready for work. Heather was getting ready for school, and she had already been in the bathtub for more than an hour. I told her several times to get out of the bathtub. Each time she gave me a flippant response. I continued coaxing her nicely so as not to upset her and trigger an episode.

I felt I was walking on eggshells with her most of the time. I never knew what would set her off, but I would go to great lengths to avoid her violent outbursts. For the fourth time I said, "Heather, get out of the tub and get dressed for school."

She responded, "Hell no. I'll get out when I'm ready."

I decided I had had enough. I stood in the bathroom doorway and said to her, "Get out now!"

She responded, "Leave me the hell alone!"

No longer willing to tolerate her verbal abuse and defiance, I physically grabbed her out of the tub and forced her into her room. Later I realized my reaction was probably not a wise one, but at the time I decided I was not going to continue to let her speak to me that way.

Heather stood naked in her room, angry that I forced her out of the bathtub. She became even more agitated and began yelling and screaming. Her face became bright red and her body was shaking. As she stood just inches from me, she had such a deep, cold look in her eyes. She spewed the most incredibly vile words at me. I stood there frozen in disbelief.

Just then she began clawing at her body, scratching her arms and hands—causing them to bleed. I continued to stand there in stunned silence, as if it were all happening in slow motion; I was unable to even move. My mind was telling me to take action, but all I could do was stand there and watch Heather violate herself.

At that moment, Steve came in the room and tried to take control of the situation. But again, this only made things worse. He demanded, "Heather, stop it!"

Instead of heeding Steve's demands, it further fueled her rage. She put both hands to her head and pulled as much hair out as her strength would allow.

I continued standing there in stunned silence.

Steve grabbed Heather's hands to stop her, but her strength was incredible. As he tried to restrain her, she just held on tighter and kept yanking, grabbing fistsful of hair with each tug. It had to be terribly painful for her, but she did not seem to notice. After a long struggle, Steve was successful in removing Heather's hands from her head. But each time he let up, she attempted to pull more hair out.

Finally, Steve had no choice but to physically restrain her. He put Heather on her stomach and lay on top of her, like a wrestler does trying to pin his opponent. As he held Heather to the ground, he had her hands behind her back, and his legs across hers so she could not kick him.

I couldn't help but think, *Isn't this how criminals are treated?*

The flurry of emotions sweeping over me was overwhelming. I was incredibly angry at the destructive nature of Heather's behavior, and at the same time, angry that we were forced to manhandle our own child.

When the situation appeared to be under control, I called Dr. Quinlen. He told us to bring Heather into the hospital for admission.

Admission? What did he mean by admission?

Although I had no idea what he thought hospitalization would do, it was a relief to have a trained professional take command of the situation.

Heather, of course, did not assist us when we told her she was being taken to the hospital. Another struggle ensued to get her in the car.

It never entered our minds to call the police for transportation. Steve and I would later learn that police are often used to escort combative patients to the emergency room, but this time we took her in ourselves.

Heather was naked as a result of just coming out of the bathtub, so we had to force her into her clothes. We faced the decision to simply haul her in the car nude or harm her or ourselves trying to get her dressed. Fortunately we were successful in getting a sweatshirt and sweatpants on her.

During the drive to the hospital, I had no idea what in-patient hospitalization meant. I kept searching for an answer to Heather's behavior. I asked myself over and over, *Where did I go wrong?*

There had to be some answer that would explain Heather's behavior. But the harder I searched, the more frustrated I became. When we arrived at the hospital emergency room, Heather stopped trying to hurt herself, but she would not talk. She held a steady, defiant gaze at anyone who dared to look her way.

After an initial examination in the emergency room, she was admitted as a patient in the mental-health unit of the hospital.

Upon admittance, Heather became combative with the nurse. She was placed into the locked quiet room, a small room with nothing in it but a bed with restraints and padded walls. Before placing Heather in the quiet room, the nurse emptied her pockets. In the quiet room, patients are not allowed to have anything that they can use to harm themselves. The room has a small window high on the door so that a child Heather's size could not see out. The nurses constantly monitor the room through a mounted camera on the ceiling.

I soon learned the meaning of a five-point restraint. Heather was placed in the bed with restraints around her arms, legs, and waist to keep her from harming herself as she thrashed around. A cold, hollow feeling entered the pit of my stomach as I watched my daughter restrained to the bed in that manner.

The next day, Heather calmed down enough to be moved to a private room with more amenities. She periodically continued her aggression, which immediately resulted in her being sent back to the quiet room for a while. Each subsequent time was shorter than the last.

During Heather's hospitalization, she was monitored constantly and had to follow a strict schedule. Any deviation from it resulted in a loss of privileges.

The daily routine included individual and group behavioral therapy sessions as well as study and chore time. Visitors were restricted to immediate family only and visiting hours were minimal and strictly enforced. Heather was not allowed to see us if she lost visiting privileges due to an outburst.

When Steve and I could visit, we usually arrived just as the group-therapy sessions were ending. During one session, as Steve and I were sitting in the waiting area, we could see a few of the patients, including Heather, through the glass enclosure. Just as I spotted Heather in the group, she sprang out of her chair, picked it up and hurled it across the room. Three staff members took her to the quiet room, and we lost our visit for the day.

I was upset that I could not see Heather and thought that the consequences were rather harsh. But the doctors and staff members insisted that if they gave in to our demands for visits, Heather would not take responsibility for her behavior.

I learned to keep quiet about my disappointment, but it was difficult. It felt like I was forced to deny my child the comfort and motherly support she needed. I began to have a greater understanding of the often overused phrase "tough love."

After two weeks, Heather was released from the hospital, before Dr. Quinlen thought she was ready. But because we had reached the maximum number of in-patient hospitalization days that our mental-health insurance plan would cover, he had no choice but to discharge her. In-patient hospital stays are not meant for long-term treatment. They are meant only to deal with immediate crisis management and a short-term stabilization period. Steve and I quickly learned that mental-health care is very limited within the health-insurance industry.

As we met with Dr. Quinlen to discuss Heather's outpatient treatment, Dr. Quinlen abruptly suggested that we put Heather in a group home—for, as he said, "a couple of years."

He added, "In my twenty-five years of working with children, I have never met a child who I felt I could not treat. But with Heather, I am at a loss. She has a chronic disturbance of affect and a need for round-the-clock treatment. She is a danger to herself and others, and I don't know how you both can take care of her and keep her and your family safe. I recommend she be placed in a residential treatment center."

He further went on to say, "Since mental health insurance will not adequately cover her needs, you need to turn to the juvenile courts because that is the only way you can gain access to mental health services. It will most likely mean you will have to give up custody of your daughter."

I could not believe what he said. How dare he suggest we just give up on Heather? And how dare he even suggest that we give up custody of Heather? I was not being a Pollyanna about the severity of Heather's problems, but I did not believe they were hopeless!

Steve and I left Dr. Quinlen's office angry and confused.

April 20, 1995

Dr. Quinlen told us we need to put Heather in an institution and that we have to give up custody! I know things are bad but I can't just give up. How could he just tell us to give up on Heather? I need to hear him tell me that there is hope. I need to hear him say that we can work this out. I can't accept this option. I don't know how much more I can take.

Once the shock of Dr. Quinlen's words wore off, Steve and I began to discuss our options for what we hoped would be the best course of treatment. While we struggled with our decision of how best to help Heather, we knew one thing for certain: We were not going to send her away or give up custody.

Instead, Steve and I explored another option that we heard of from Ms. Parker, a day program called the outpatient-partial program offered through one of the local mental-health centers.

The outpatient-partial program, as the name implies, is a hospitalization program on a partial, outpatient basis. It is a day program that provides a complete range of services, such as behavioral and cognitive therapy, medical and mental health treatment, and educational and living skills training. Heather would attend the day program on regular school days and be home with us on evenings and weekends.

The program has an array of professional staff consisting of trained therapists, nurses, doctors, and educators—all specialized in child behavior disorders—that provide one-on-one treatment for the child, based on a custom plan designed to fit her specific needs.

As a school-age child, it was important that Heather continued to get her education. But education is secondary to social and behavioral development.

The day program focused on the medical and mental-health aspects of Heather's treatment program while ensuring that her educational needs were not overlooked.

Steve and I wanted Heather at home where she would have the love and support of her family. We felt that no institution could provide that. Yet we also knew Heather needed an environment like the outpatient-partial program during the day in order to continue receiving educational and therapeutic services. After hearing about the program from Ms. Parker, I called and set up an appointment to speak with the program's administrator.

During our meeting, I learned that our insurance would cover the mental-health aspect of the program, but the school district would have to cover the educational portion. Steve and I were elated to find what appeared to be a great solution.

We presented all the information to the principal and requested that the school district provide for Heather's education through the day program. We quickly found out the school district was not as ecstatic about this option as we were.

The educational expenses associated with the day program were not small, and we still had the problem of Heather being in Level I special-education placement. The day program is a Level III, out-of-school placement, and with Heather still at Level I at her local school, it became apparent we were asking the impossible—to jump from Level I to Level III.

I soon got the sense that we were swimming upstream when our request was flatly denied. The director of the school district's special-education services told us we had not exhausted all options at Level I to warrant such a drastic move.

With their denial, Steve and I had no other choice but to wait and hope Heather's behavior would stabilize.

Dr. Quinlen's recommendation also presented another problem; Steve and I felt we had to find another doctor to treat Heather. Dr. Quinlen did not come out and say he would not treat her, but his stated doubt about his ability to work with her did not give us any comfort.

When we petitioned our health maintenance organization (HMO) plan to switch doctors, the HMO administrator perceived our request as our unwillingness to work with the doctor. This attitude was further evidenced by the lecture we received from the administrator. Upon scheduling our first visit with our new doctor, the administrator said, "You better hope this new doctor works for you because this is the last time you can switch."

Heather's new psychiatrist, Dr. Johns, came highly recommended from Ms. Parker. During the initial meeting with Dr. Johns, I expressed to him my concern that Heather might be suffering from bipolar. The more erratic and persistent Heather's behavior grew, the more convinced I was that she might be suffering from this disorder.

Because he did not know us too well, I don't think Dr. Johns felt comfortable with our assessment. When he shrugged off my suggestion, I urged him once more to consider the possibility. I know I probably came off as an overbearing mother, but by this time, I did not care. I just wanted him to consider our input. Instead, he continued Heather on her current medications.

Shortly after Heather's discharge from the hospital, we spent one morning at my sister-in-law's for a birthday party. She lived about fifty miles away, so the drive was just under an hour. During the party, Heather became agitated and restless with the other kids and was unruly and defiant with me. I had to separate her from the other kids several times.

In frustration, we left the party early. On the way home, Heather began to torment her brothers, pushing their buttons in ways she knew would make them respond. Soon she had each of them angry with her, anxious to be home to escape the entrapment of the car that forced them to have to put up with her retorts.

Our sons realized early on with Heather that sometimes the best thing to do was just sit there and not say anything. So that is what they did. The silence was a relief, but short-lived. Within a few minutes, I was alerted to the sound of the wind whirling loudly from the backseat. From the corner of my eye I saw Heather grab for the door handle. She opened the back car door and attempted to jump out!

Instinctively I reached back and grabbed her arm—just before she got her foot out of the car. Panic set in and mobilized me to action. In desperation, I asked Michael to hold the car door closed while I maneuvered my way to the backseat.

Steve was trying to keep the car on the road as I quickly jumped in the backseat. As I reached the back, Heather and Michael were in a tug-of-war, Heather trying to get hold of the door handle, hell-bent on opening it. I sat on Heather, hoping to pin her down long enough to take command of the situation. As I sat on her, she continued to grab for the car door handle.

"Heather, please don't do this," I begged her. "You'll kill yourself."

The more I begged, the harder she tried to free herself.

All of a sudden Heather stopped struggling with me, looked me squarely in the eyes, and said, "Let me die."

She freed her left hand from my grip and, once again, grabbed the car door, swinging it open. Since I had my back against the door, I nearly lost my balance. I could feel the wind rushing through my shirt. Because both my hands were tied up trying to hold on to Heather, I yelled for Michael to close the door. After a minute he was finally able to squeeze by the two of us and grab hold of the handle to shut the door. With the second failed attempt to jump out of the car, Heather seemed to have lost her steam, and she gave up the fight. Her body, rigid and tight during the struggle, went limp.

I cradled her and began to realize how precariously close she had come to fulfilling her wish to die. She continued to let me hold her but seemed angry with me—angry that she didn't succeed.

Just then Steve had stopped the car and pulled over to the side of the road. We pondered what to do next. What do you do in the middle of the highway with a child who is trying to jump out of a moving vehicle going sixty miles per hour?

We did not have a cell phone to call for help. The only way to get home was to continue driving, so we waited another ten minutes to make sure Heather was still calm. But I could not count on her to continue sitting there without trying it again. I sat on her for the rest of the ride home. It was the only solution I could think of. Passers-by gave us questioning stares, and I'm sure this seemed odd to them, but at the time, I didn't care.

I was trying to maintain my composure externally, while internally my mind was whirling in desperation, asking myself over and over again, *Why would Heather want to kill herself?*

After this event, Dr. Johns realized that Heather's current medications were not doing any good. I honestly thought the medications were increasing Heather's impulsivity and volatility. I told Dr. Johns this and asked him again if he would consider trying something for bipolar.

Instead he put Heather on Risperidone, a drug used to control psychotic thinking. Psychosis can lead a patient to have hallucinations or be delusional. Like Ritalin, Risperidone seemed to have absolutely no positive effect on Heather. In fact, her behavior only continued to worsen.

Part Four:
Descent into the Abyss

The Summer of '95

In the summer of 1995, Heather's behavior took a radical turn for the worse. It was all-consuming. I became concerned for the safety of my family. I feared that if we did not get an answer to Heather's volatile behavior soon, the chances of something drastic happening were high.

Eventually, my family became isolated, as we could not engage in "normal" everyday activities. Fear of what might happen next consumed my every waking moment, and I was constantly on pins and needles. If I wasn't dealing with one of Heather's erratic mood swings, I was dreading and preparing myself for the next.

Looking back, I often ask myself, *How did we do it?* To this day I do not know how we survived this experience. There were days I wanted to walk away from the bleakness of our circumstances. Sheer determination, tenacity, and faith in God got us through.

Because of the summer break, Steve and I had to find day care for Heather. This obstacle was so daunting that we seriously considered one of us taking a leave of absence from work, but that was not an option we could afford. So each day, we hung onto whatever sense of survival and hope we had. Besides, staying home with Heather would not provide the solution to the problem. Heather needed to be treated by professionals, but I was still torn inside between staying home and working. Part of that struggle came from the frequent sting of subtle, yet obvious, comments from other parents who implied that if we just gave Heather more of our time, she would be all right.

I felt that my work was one aspect of my life over which I had control, and it provided a respite from Heather's aggression. I was emphatic that I was not going to be pulled down into the darkness of Heather's behavior. If Steve or I did, our family might fall apart.

We began the process of finding a good summer day care program. Through it all, God has always provided the right people at the right time during our journey. He did not let us down this time.

We were fortunate to meet with the director of the local Salvation Army summer program, Ms. Combs. She was in college, majoring in special education for behaviorally disturbed children. With her experience and education, Ms. Combs agreed to work with Heather. I had high hopes that this was the place where Heather would be able to thrive. Unfortunately, my hopes were dashed all too soon.

Within no time, Heather's usual defiant, angry outbursts exceeded the ability of the caregivers. Many days, when Heather became too combative, the staff called me to pick her up early. After one episode, I was distraught and at my wits' end. I do not know why but I asked Ms. Combs, "If I didn't know Heather, and you had to describe her to me, what would you say?"

Ms. Combs stated, "Heather is highly intelligent and aware of her environment. When she is under control, she is a pleasure to be around. She can be very attentive and helpful with the other kids and staff."

Ms. Combs shifted in her chair and added, "But when she becomes edgy, she will become very manipulative. If she cannot manipulate the situation her way, she will become aggressive. If initial aggressive behavior is not successful in manipulating the situation, her aggression will eventually escalate to the point of danger, if not controlled."

I was amazed! Ms. Combs clearly described the typical pattern of behavior that Heather exhibited beginning at nineteen months of age! Why did she see it when others didn't?

After two more weeks, Heather still did not improve at the day care, so we pulled her out.

July 19, 1995

I took Heather out of the summer program. They didn't ask me to but I know it's just a matter of time before they do. I really hoped this place would work. Ms. Combs tried hard. Most people want to rid themselves of Heather and then pass judgment about my parenting. But Ms. Combs wasn't that way. It felt good to have someone who doesn't patronize me. She really seems to understand that all we want is to find an answer.

My father offered to take Mark and Heather for the rest of the summer. I was hesitant, but I hoped that the change of scenery and being with her grandparents would be a positive step for Heather. My father and stepmom lived about four hours away in a small town in Iowa. We drove up the next day. I tried to prepare my father for Heather's behavior, but he, like many others who first heard about Heather's behavior, told me to stop worrying so much.

Because Michael was in Arizona with his godparents and Heather and Mark were with their grandparents, Steve and I looked forward to three weeks alone. We desperately needed time together after so many years of struggling with Heather's continual and escalating behavior.

While Steve and I were enjoying our first few days alone, Heather's aggression and defiance came to a head. I called my father in the middle of the first week. A few times during the conversation I suspected something was bothering him. He kept starting to ask a question, but stopped midsentence. I ended the conversation with the understanding that we would pick up the kids in a couple of weeks.

Over the next two and a half weeks Steve and I were carefree. We ate out many nights at the finer restaurants, went to the movies often and even went on a five-day trip throughout Nebraska—horseback riding, canoeing, and fishing, while staying at several bed-and-breakfasts. Our time alone went by too fast and before long we were heading to my father's to pick up the kids.

When we arrived in town, I stopped to buy a flower arrangement for my stepmom. As we pulled up to my father's house, my stepmother greeted us at the door. As I raised the flower basket toward her, she looked at me and then at the flowers and said, "That isn't going to make it better. You'll need a lot more than that!"

Stunned, I asked her, "What do you mean?" She instantly proceeded to tell me what a horrible daughter I had. Her comments stung as she did not mince words in telling me how terrible Heather's behavior was. Hard as it was, I was able to contain my initial response. My father walked in and could sense the tension between us. He intervened early enough to neutralize what could have become an ugly confrontation. After a few minutes, we all sat down and talked for quite a while.

My stepmom described the time when Heather broke her favorite rocking chair in a fit of rage and the frequent complaints Heather made about the meals my stepmom worked so hard to prepare. I was embarrassed as they described the problems they encountered with Heather. I realized that my father and his wife could not understand the full scope of what we were dealing with, so I tempered my feelings of humiliation. My father and stepmother, after all, were totally unprepared for what they had to deal with. After this experience, Steve and I ceased most contact with our extended family.

August 23, 1995

I was so humiliated today. I know my dad and his wife weren't trying to be mean, but their comments hurt like hell. All I could think about on the way home was, How can I ever face them again?

At the end of the summer, just before Heather's tenth birthday, Dr. Johns switched Heather's medications again. He prescribed Prozac, an antidepressant. I asked him why he was switching her medications and he said, "Sometimes it takes a lot of trial and error to find the right medication."

I was frustrated with his lack of certainty, but I later learned just how hard it was to find the right medication. After Heather's attempt to jump out of the car, I began doing my own research on behavior disorders.

I spent a lot of time in the public library, reading numerous books on childhood development and mental illness. Much of what I read was frightening and overwhelming, but I continued trudging through the different material, hoping to find the one clue that would answer all of my questions.

I will never profess to be an expert on mental illness, but I know Heather. I knew something was wrong. As a mother, I could not stand around doing nothing. I am a pragmatic person. I looked at our plight with the philosophy, "If there's a problem, let's find out what it is and do what it takes to fix it."

I became more convinced that Heather had a high chance of suffering from bipolar. Since Dr. Johns was already going to change Heather's medications, I asked him to try something for bipolar. I reminded Dr. Johns about the history of bipolar in my family in the hopes that he would see a connection. I had absolute trust in my feelings and beliefs that Heather was afflicted with bipolar, but our culture places little or no value on inner knowledge or intuition. I urged him to try this medication, if for nothing else but to rule it out. Dr. Johns responded, "Bipolar is not typically found in children."

About a month before Heather started fifth grade, Steve and I moved into a new home. We had been renting a house in a nice neighborhood, but the area was too congested. After living in the crowded cities of southern California for so long, we longed for wide open spaces. The house we were hoping to purchase was outside the city—with farms and a lake surrounding it. Unfortunately, the home was not located in the same school district the kids were currently attending. Steve and I did not make a commitment on the new house until we could be sure that changing school districts would not have any adverse impact on Heather's special-education support.

I placed a call to the principal of the new school to ask about the special-education services. She told me that all of the school districts follow the child's established IEP (Individual Education Program). Armed with that information, Steve and I bought the house and moved our family at the end of July.

A week before school started, Steve and I met with the school principal and Heather's teacher to introduce ourselves and discuss Heather's special-education plan. We gave them copies of Heather's psychological evaluation and IEP plan from the previous school district. We also inquired about the outpatient-partial program in the hopes they would recommend that option, but they did not. The next week Heather started her new school, and much to my surprise, she was placed full-time in the mainstream classroom.

Without the structure and training that a special-education classroom provides, Heather had little chance to succeed. Within a short time her behavior problems were evident. Heather received her first suspension in the second week of school. Steve and I used this event as a basis for requesting treatment for Heather in the outpatient-partial program. With Heather's problematic behavior right from the start, we knew the school environment could not meet Heather's mental and educational needs. I did not want another year of continual suspensions for Heather and parent bashing toward us by the educators. We hoped for a positive outcome to our request, but it was flatly denied.

Special education is expensive; therefore, a history has to be documented, and all other alternatives must be exhausted before escalation is exercised. I understand that the school district needed to make certain that a clear case existed before further support was provided, but in Heather's case, I felt that there was a definite pattern of escalating behavior and compelling medical documentation to warrant her placement into the outpatient-partial program. This bureaucracy was maddening.

The situation was a ticking time bomb. With each new episode, Heather expanded the boundaries of her aggression until I often asked them, "What has to happen before someone will do something?"

Another week and a half went by and Heather was suspended again due to a serious outburst in the classroom, where she struck another child. With this suspension, Steve and I felt we could no longer sit idly by and wait for the school district to do something, so we hired an attorney to assist us in getting Heather in the proper setting.

Through our attorney, Ms. Calkins, we petitioned the school district for special-education placement in the outpatient-partial program. We felt the school's lack of special-education support put Heather's safety and the safety of others at stake. This was a difficult decision for Steve and me because we wanted to resolve this matter in a positive, cooperative way. However, we were gravely concerned for the safety of Heather and other students. Not so selflessly, we were also concerned about our risk of liability. With the level of Heather's volatility, it was not unthinkable that she could injure, albeit unintentionally, another student, or cause extensive property damage to the school. Since the school district was unwilling to consider the history of Heather's behavior and heed the advice of the reams of medical documentation, we felt we were left with little recourse.

Ms. Calkins presented the petition to the school district, and within one week we were told that it was denied. The school district's legal team far outweighed the resources Steve and I could throw at this problem. We had to continue playing what I felt was a wait-and-see game. Although I was not naïve enough to think that the day program was an immediate cure, I knew Heather would only worsen in her present environment.

September 13, 1995

God, this is maddening! Heather is out of control most of the time and the school's pat answer is to suspend her. I don't know how to make the administrators see that she needs help. I'm so afraid that she will get so out of control that they can't handle it. She could hurt herself or someone else. What do I have to do to make them see that?

A Cyclical History of Hospitalization

One evening in late October, as Steve and I were taking Heather to an appointment with her therapist, she became combative. As Steve pulled into the parking lot and stopped the car, Heather opened the door and bolted toward the street. I yelled for Steve to run after her. He caught up with her a couple blocks away and a struggle ensued. In the meantime, I ran into the building for help.

Three security guards came to assist Steve. Two guards held onto Heather's arms while the third held onto her legs. Before the guard could grab her legs she kicked him squarely in the face. Hurt, but refusing to give in, the guard reached for Heather's legs, making sure he did not get kicked again.

As soon as they had a firm hold on her, they put her to the ground—face down with her hands held tightly behind her back. One of the guards yelled at the nurse standing outside, "Get me a boat!"

I thought, *A boat? What's a boat?*

Then someone came out carrying a cage-like device shaped like a small boat with straps on the top. In one fell swoop the guards unceremoniously swung Heather into the device and fastened the straps. Heather's screams could not be ignored as she demanded, "Get me the hell out of here!"

It was horrifying to witness her wild struggles while she was literally shoved into the device. In the background, I was crying and begging them to stop, but obviously they could not pay any attention to me.

Heather was taken to the emergency room and given a shot of Thorazine, a tranquilizer. Within a few minutes, it began to take effect, and Heather stopped struggling. As she quietly lay on the gurney, I was torn between wanting to take her over my knee and spank her for her "bad" behavior, or holding her in my arms in the hopes that my love would melt away her rage. When our eyes met, she turned her head away from me in defiance.

Eventually she fell into a drug-induced sleep. I walked over to her and held her hand and tried not to cry as the tears filled my eyes.

In the emergency room, Dr. Johns was called to assess Heather. He decided to admit her into the hospital for in-patient treatment. This was Heather's second mental-health inpatient stay in six months. After her first hospitalization earlier in the year, I had hoped it would be her last.

Heather remained in the hospital for five days. I began to see a change in her demeanor. She almost seemed relaxed. I could not pinpoint why—perhaps it was because she did not have to put on a facade while in the hospital. All her peers on the ward were there for reasons similar to hers, and it might have provided comfort to her to know that she was not the only child struggling with problems of extreme behavior and the effects of her roller-coaster moods.

Heather had been home for only three weeks when, in late November, she became out of control again, and in a fit of rage, started pounding her fist against the big plateglass window in the kitchen. Steve grabbed her hands for fear she would break through the glass. As he held her from behind, with her arms wrapped against her chest, she bit his hand. When Steve jerked back, he accidentally hit Heather on the head.

Heather screamed, "You hit me, that's child abuse! I'm going to call the police and tell them you are abusing me."

Steve responded, "You know I do not abuse you."

Heather broke free, spun around and spat in his face and yelled, "Screw you. I'm calling the police."

She reached for the phone and dialed 911.

She told the operator, "Come right away. My father is abusing me."

I had to fight the urge to grab the phone from her, but I was afraid if I did, the police might think that we had something to hide.

The dispatcher told Heather someone would be there soon.

She smugly hung up the phone, turned to Steve and said, "They are coming here. I hope you are ready to go to jail."

I said to her, "Heather, I hope you are prepared for whatever happens. You know your father has never abused you. Your false accusations will not be taken lightly by the police."

Even though there was no truth to her accusations, it was unsettling to be falsely accused of child abuse—especially by our own child.

Twenty minutes went by and still there were no police. I began to wonder if they were going to come. With the delay, Heather began to realize she had made a mistake.

She asked me, "Can I call them back and tell them it's okay, they don't need to come?"

I replied, "No, Heather, they have to respond. You have to realize that you can't say things like that and then take them back when you calm down. You made the call, you will have to deal with whatever happens."

Within another ten minutes, two deputy sheriffs arrived. Immediately one deputy took Heather upstairs and the other met with Steve and me. They asked all three of us to give our sides of the story. The deputy meeting with us left to speak with Heather and the other officer.

As the deputies asked Heather for more information about her accusations, she became uncooperative. The more they prodded her to explain the incident, the more defiant and belligerent she became. She started cursing at them and then in a fit of anger, she tried to kick one of them. As she became more agitated, she began to get physically aggressive with them, forcing the officers to have to restrain her. She became so combative that they decided to take her to the hospital emergency room. Once there, Heather was given a shot of Thorazine and Dr. Johns, once again, placed her as an in-patient for observation.

During this hospitalization, Dr. Johns felt that Heather was not able to go back to the public school. This was Heather's third hospitalization in seven months. She was clearly not capable of managing herself in a school setting. Her level of dysfunction was becoming greater each day. Dr. Johns insisted that Heather be placed in the out-patient-partial program for three to four weeks for additional support and therapy.

When he suggested this, I explained to him our numerous unsuccessful efforts to get the school district to support this option. But where Steve and I were unsuccessful, Dr. Johns succeeded. With his advice, the school agreed to pay for the educational component of the outpatient-partial program for a limited period.

On November 28, 1995, Heather was transferred to the out-patient-partial program. I knew she would not be happy about the day program, not just because it meant meeting new people, but also because she did not like the institution-like atmosphere. I could not blame her. The facility was a mental-health center and resided in the same building as the hospital. The classrooms and therapy rooms were decorated to give the feel of school, but there was no denying that it was not a typical school.

The day program is a rigidly structured behavioral-therapy program in which the children earn points for positive behavior and lose them for negative behavior. Based on their points, they are given varying levels of privileges. On Heather's first day of the program, she made her displeasure known immediately and lost all of her privileges.

During the first week of December, Steve and I took the day off from work to do some Christmas shopping and spend some time alone. The day went by fast, and before we were ready, it was time to pick up Heather from the day program. Once we arrived, Steve waited in the car while I went inside to pick up Heather. As I approached her, she gave me a surly look that indicated she was not in the best of moods.

Upbeat from the holiday festivities, I was determined not to let Heather's surly demeanor destroy my peace. The drive home was quiet, as I sensed it was best not to interact with Heather too much. I hoped the festive Christmas music on the radio would give her time to wind down and change her outlook to a more positive one. When we got home, Heather immediately went to her room, slamming her door behind her.

As I cooked dinner, Steve and the boys went downstairs to watch TV. Once dinner was ready, I called everyone to the table. Steve and the boys came right away. After ten minutes, Heather was still in her bedroom. I called up to her, but she still did not respond. Finally, I went up to her bedroom. As I opened her door, she gave me a look of displeasure, but fortunately, she quietly came downstairs to join us for dinner.

The minute she entered the dining room and saw what we were having she said, "You know I don't like fish."

I responded, "I put a lemon sauce on it that I think you will like; just try it."

She rolled her eyes at me as if to say, "Yeah, right."

I ignored her and silently hoped she would not make a big deal out of it. The boys kept their eyes glued to their plates and did not make eye contact with her. I was thankful when she quietly dished up her plate and began eating. With her first bite of fish she puckered up her mouth, spit the food out into her napkin, and exclaimed,

"This is the worst damn fish I've ever had!"

"Go to your room," I told her.

Heather picked up her chair and threw it across the dining room.

Steve stood and moved toward Heather in case she continued her tirade. Just then, Heather retreated to her room. As Steve moved to go after her I said to him, "Leave her alone for a while. Maybe she will calm down."

All was quiet in Heather's room—and I thought we had succeeded in avoiding a confrontation, but no sooner had this thought crossed my mind than I heard a loud crash. I ran upstairs to find Heather throwing her books against her dresser.

I yelled at Steve to call the police. Heather did not act like she was going to calm down anytime soon. Many times it was impossible to know at what point to call the police. Steve and I decided that if we made a mistake, we would rather err on the side of caution.

In a rage, Heather's behavior could escalate within seconds. Heather pushed me out of the doorway and slammed her door shut. I stood outside listening intently to what was going on inside her bedroom, ready to respond if needed. I heard Heather moving something. Every few minutes I asked her, "Heather, are you okay in there?"

Each time she responded, "Leave me the hell alone!"

Even though I knew my questions made her angry, I kept asking her until she would respond. I took her response as a good sign that she was not harming herself.

Within five minutes, two sheriffs arrived. I could hear Steve downstairs talking with them, and after a few minutes I went downstairs to join them. As they discussed how to best approach Heather, I offered to try to talk her into coming out of her room. I walked back upstairs and asked Heather to let me in. There was no response. I turned her doorknob slowly and proceeded to open the door, but it would only open about an inch. When I pushed it a second time, the door opened and a loud crashing sound came from the room.

Immediately Heather yelled at me, "Get out of my room, you bitch!"

The officers came rushing upstairs. They pushed me out of the way and raced into Heather's bedroom.

Heather had barricaded her door with the bookshelf in her room and when I tried to open the door, it came crashing down. That, coupled with Heather's yelling, made the officers jump into action.

As they stumbled over the bookshelf, Heather stood at the foot of the bed, cursing at the officers. One of them grabbed her by the arm and threw her onto the bed. With her face pressed to the mattress, he pulled her hands behind her back.

"Why do you have to be so rough?" I asked.

"This is how we handle it," the officer said.

Heather had to be carried to the police cruiser and taken to the emergency room. After a brief time there, she was admitted to the psychiatric ward. For the third time in as many months, and the fourth time in eight months, Heather was hospitalized.

She stayed in the hospital this time for four days, and upon discharge, went back to the day program. She resumed the program until the end of the semester when the school contract expired.

Before school resumed after Christmas break, we asked the school district to extend the contract for the outpatient-partial program. In light of Heather's additional in-patient stay we thought surely it would be accepted. We were wrong. Instead, Heather was transferred to another school. A transfer was required for special-education support because only select schools have the staff to manage the needs of severe special-education students. Steve and I were very angry about this decision. Forcing the move meant Heather had to endure another unnecessary adjustment.

I worried that a move to another school would only cause more traumas for Heather, which in turn caused her to become more combative. Heather had been tossed around like a yo-yo for the last two years. We urged the school district to keep Heather in the outpatient-partial program, but the special education administrator denied our request. Feeling we had no other choice, Steve and I gave into the demands of this bureaucracy. As a result, Heather was bused each day to a school well out of our neighborhood—with a new set of teachers and peers.

The move was a disaster from the start. Heather's outbursts and suspensions occurred almost immediately. We wasted no time in requesting placement back at the outpatient-partial program. Each time our request was denied.

Some days I wondered if we would ever get an answer to Heather's behavior and be able to live a normal life. During the tumultuous eight-year struggle of dealing with Heather's extreme behavior,

I felt so inadequate many times, particularly because I believed as a Christian that God would not allow bad things to happen to good people. I struggled to understand why God would allow such a terrible illness to befall my little girl and cause such anguish for my family.

One Saturday following a particularly challenging week, Steve and I were invited to his sister and brother-in-law's home for a visit. As Steve and I shared our frustration over Heather's recent suspension, they did not offer the typical advice others usually did—take parenting classes or just be more firm with her. Instead, Steve's sister said to us, "God gave Heather to you two for a reason. He knows you both can handle it and will use this illness to his good."

Her words helped me to realize that God was not punishing us, but that he is there for us at the times our strength is diminished and to understand that his greater plan for us, while difficult to endure, would get us through this. Her comforting words were what I needed at the time and gave me the strength to keep going.

As Heather's aggressive outbursts continued, the school's automatic response—suspension from school—was a typical example of their inability to understand the gravity of Heather's situation. With each suspension, Steve and I used the incident to once again impress upon the school principal the need for additional support that the outpatient-partial program could provide. Yet each time, the school district denied our request. I am sure they were tired of our requests as much as we were tired of asking and being denied. I felt like they thought Heather's problems were entirely our fault. This belief was evident when one day, after Heather spat in the special-education teacher's face, she said to me, "Can't you just control your child?"

With Heather's behavior, I soon learned that control is not what you can demand from her but what she chooses to give. And control is based on Heather's boundaries of reality. I later learned how Heather, struggling with the effects of improperly treated mental illness, had a distorted sense of reality. The more I tried to explain to the teacher that Heather needed medical and psychiatric help, the more she judged me as an incompetent mother.

A special-education classroom involves the use of a trained

instructor who specializes in behavior disorders. The class size is significantly smaller than the regular classroom. The ratio is typically one teacher, plus a teacher's aide, to five or six students. The class setting is rigidly structured and the schedule strictly adhered to. Any hint of improper behavior is supposed to be dealt with immediately. This type of class environment was a shock for Heather.

In this classroom, Heather was not always the one acting out. She got to witness other children's extreme behaviors. One night Heather expressed amazement at another student's behavior in class. She thought it was incredible. I did not point out to her that the behavior she described of her classmate could also describe hers. This is why parenting Heather is so difficult. When untreated, Heather does not see her actions in the way they really happen. During a manic cycle, Heather's response is typically to blame others for her actions, often stating, "He made me mad so I had to hit him"; to minimize the situation by saying something like, "I didn't hit him that hard"; and to deny any responsibility for her actions. This type of thinking is maddening for a parent to deal with. Too many times I felt inadequate to be an effective parent to Heather.

In January 1996, Heather was admitted for inpatient hospitalization again. With this hospitalization, her fifth in nine months, we were quickly becoming regulars by the staff's standards. By now, I was very familiar with the intake routine. But this time was completely different.

The nurse, whom I had never met, immediately began a line of questions aimed directly at me, even though Steve was right by my side. She first asked, "Mrs. Byers, do you work?"

When I responded yes, she followed up with, "Hmm, that's interesting."

She then asked me, "How much time do you spend with your daughter?" I answered her question and she sarcastically asked me, "Are you sure you spend enough time with her?"

I squirmed in my seat. Then she asked, "Mrs. Byers, how do you discipline Heather?" I answered her and she again replied with some flippant response laced with judgmental overtones.

By now Steve could see that I was upset, so he stopped the interview. But it was too late. I read the implication of these questions and the suggestion that I had something to do with Heather's reason for being there. I had enough guilt of my own that the nurse's insinuations only fed them.

After Heather was settled in her room and we said our good-byes, we quietly walked to the car. It was not until we were in the car that I broke down and cried out to Steve, "Am I really a bad mother?"

January 9, 1996

Heather was put into the hospital again today. Each time this happens I feel like a part of me is being ripped open. The emotions going through my mind leave me confused and unable to concentrate. I can't think—I only feel. I feel pain, frustration and guilt. Guilt is the one emotion that doesn't need much prompting and boy, did the nurse push that button today. Maybe I deserve to be punished, but I don't want Heather to be punished. God, please help me get past the blaming and on to finding the answers and doing something to get out of this mess!

The next day when I came to visit Heather, I learned she had spent the previous night in the locked quiet room. I tried to talk with her, but she was despondent. So I numbly carried on a one-sided conversation.

We both sat on the floor beside her bed. Heather held her knees close to her chest, rocking back and forth, staring blankly at the wall. I had my arm around her shoulder, stroking her hair.

After a few minutes Heather said, "Mom, the pain is so bad I want it to go away. I wish someone would kill me."

I gasped. I put both arms around Heather and said, "Heather, hang on! Please don't give up."

At times like this, I could not understand the depth of Heather's emotions—from manic-induced rage to such depressive lows—that made suicide look like the only escape. As I held her tightly I said, "Heather, I love you so much."

I looked into her eyes, but she looked right past me. My words just went into thin air. It was agonizing not being able to help her. I held Heather tightly and rocked her. We must have sat there for well over an hour until the nurse entered the room to give Heather her medications.

I reported Heather's comment to the nurse, and they put her on suicide watch for the remainder of her hospitalization.

Heather was just over ten years old, and by now, most days she had some sort of problems that we dealt with. Steve and I measured a good day by how few times she became out of control.

After two months of continual problems at school, one day in early February, Heather had an incident that made the school officials finally realize they could not deal with her extreme behavior.

During the first hour, Heather became agitated and ran out of the classroom. Before a staff member could catch up to her, Heather raced into the girls' bathroom on the second floor. When Heather reached the bathroom, she climbed up to the window and perched herself there with only a thin screen to protect her, threatening to jump. Fortunately, after much coaxing, the staff were able to get Heather down from the window.

Heather was sent to the nurse's office while the principal called me at work. The principal told me what happened and informed me that Heather was being suspended. She then asked me to come pick her up from school. When the principal told me Heather was being suspended, I became livid!

Heather could have jumped from a two-story window and their response was to suspend her! Heather did not need suspension—she needed professional help!

I struggled to maintain my calm as I told the principal, "I will speak with my husband first and call you back in a few minutes."

She asked me, "Why do you need to call me back? Just come pick up your child!"

I tersely replied, "Since the school district continues to ignore any advice regarding our daughter's treatment needs, you deal with her."

At first the principal did not respond to what I said. I'm sure she was flabbergasted at my apparent disregard, but I was tired of being treated like a puppet.

After a long pause, the principal inquired, "Are you saying you aren't going to pick up Heather?"

I replied, "No, I'm not. I will pick Heather up at the end of the day."

I hung up the phone, shaking and upset at what I had just done. I called Steve at work and told him of the incident. I was afraid he would be mad at me. We talked a little and then agreed he would pick up Heather from school.

After I hung up, I sat at my desk, too numb to think. Not even five minutes had passed when Steve called me back to tell me that he, too, had decided not to pick Heather up from school; as he walked to his car, he had changed his mind.

He, like I, was tired of feeling like we had no say in the outcome of Heather's circumstances. Steve and I knew we were taking a big risk in refusing to pick up Heather, but we were tired of just sitting around waiting for the school administrators to do something. Heather could have jumped or fallen from the window and the staff seemed to treat it with the same consideration you would for a minor infraction.

Looking back now, I can't believe Steve and I were so bold, but we were both feeling very desperate. Fearing the consequences of our actions from the juvenile authorities, Steve and I called our attorney to inform her of our decision. I thought she might encourage us to reconsider but she, surprisingly, did not. She did, however, advise us to call the principal and demand an emergency petition hearing for Heather's placement into the day program.

I called the principal to request a meeting and informed her that our lawyer would be present. The meeting was set for the next morning.

The tone of the meeting was completely different from past meetings. Within the first five minutes, the director of special-education services agreed to Heather's placement in the outpatient-partial program! I believe the incident of the previous day had finally made the administrators aware of the seriousness of the situation. It took a few minutes for the reality of what the director had said to sink in. Finally, Heather would be in a place during the day where she could be safely cared for and given the therapy she needed until proper diagnosis and effective treatment could begin!

A huge weight was lifted from my shoulders. I could at least feel comfortable during the day in the knowledge that Heather was safe and secure.

It took a few days to complete the paperwork and process Heather into the day program. I knew this was the right move. With Heather secured, once again, we had proper care for her during the day. Steve and I hoped intense therapy would lessen the severity of Heather's mood swings and volatile behavior at home.

It helped a little at first, but not for long. Many times I felt like I was leading a double life. I would go to work and experience "normal" interactions and then go home, wondering what the next episode was going to be or if we were going to end up in the hospital that night.

The impact of this illness played a different role for each person in my family. Michael, being the oldest, learned quickly how not to be manipulated by her. He seemed to be the only one in our family that Heather did not get combative with. This caused Michael to mature beyond his years. Many times, especially when Steve was not at home and I was left to deal with Heather, Michael would step into the parental role. This caused a lot of concern for me because I did not want him to have to assume this responsibility. I wanted him and Heather to have a healthy sibling relationship. Michael was supposed to take care of Heather when the school bullies picked on her—just like my older brother did for me. I never imagined he would feel like he had to protect me from his own sister.

Heather got combative with Steve sometimes, but she targeted most of her aggression to me or to Mark. There were many times where I had to intervene when Heather was either verbally or physically assaulting Mark. It finally got to the point that we could not leave the two alone for concern for Mark's safety. It also got to the point that my relationship with Heather was becoming very strained because of her aggression toward me.

A week after Heather went back to the day program in early February 1996, Dr. Johns switched her medication to Thorazine, or as I refer to it, the drug from hell. We were certainly familiar with this drug, as it was commonly given to Heather when she was taken to the emergency room for crisis management. When I shared my concern with Dr. Johns about the recurring use of Thorazine, he assured me it was the proper medication to treat Heather's psychotic symptoms. I reluctantly accepted his advice; however, I felt its only use was to knock Heather out when all other efforts at restraining her failed.

Within days, Heather became a complete zombie. The medication kept her mildly sedated to a point where she did not have the energy to be aggressive. After a few weeks, though, Heather was "breaking through" the medications, and it took increasingly higher dosages to control her.

Instead of displaying aggressive behavior, Heather spent

most days in a semistuporous state. She slept almost twenty hours a day during the weekend. She often held her head down and did not engage in conversation or participate with the family unless we urged her. Even then, her concentration was limited.

Eventually, Steve and I asked Dr. Johns to take Heather off this medication. I would rather deal with Heather's aggression than see her in a constant drugged state. I really felt this drug was the lazy way for the doctors and therapist to deal with the problem—knock her out so she would not bother anyone.

I'm not trying to be overly critical of the doctors. The severity of Heather's aggression gave the professionals little recourse. As it became increasingly more difficult to keep our family safe, we too gained some respite from this drug. But it should have only been used as a temporary measure.

It was not until Heather's caseworker intervened a few months later, after seeing Heather so heavily sedated, that Dr. Johns took her off this medication.

Because of the volatile behavior Heather exhibited during a manic episode, we were forced to turn our house into a hospital-like setting. Sharp objects and knickknacks were removed to prevent Heather from using them during an episode. We even boarded up Heather's bedroom windows for a short period, so she would not break them as she often pounded on them. We were often patching walls and replacing doors, furniture, or carpet. We also set up a time-out room for Heather. This was an isolated, secured location in the house, where Heather was sent when she was out of control. She could sit in the room for as long as she needed to calm down. It was preferable for her to voluntarily go there, even if it was for hours, than to deal with her explosive outbursts. Turning our home into this kind of environment went against everything inside me. A home is supposed to be a soft, warm place. Our home felt more like an institution. We no longer invited people over. It was too embarrassing.

Steve and I spent less and less time together. The tender moments we shared were overshadowed by the time and energy it took to deal with Heather's behavior. I constantly feared and worried, *What's going to happen next?* Day by day, the moments of intimacy were robbed from us. Soon our lives became a daily chore. I began to wonder if there would be a light at the end of the tunnel. I even considered just walking away.

This scared me. I never considered myself a quitter, but I honestly began to wonder if we were ever going to get through this. Buried beneath the drudgery of our daily life, I clung to the belief that God had not forsaken us.

Days and weeks passed with no relief in sight from the effects of Heather's volatility. My nerves were becoming extremely raw. One evening, shortly after dinner, Heather became abusive with me, but fortunately she heeded Steve's recommendation to go to her time-out room before things got worse. Even though Heather calmed down without assistance, I was still upset. The tension was becoming unbearable.

After Heather left the room, I approached Steve and said, "I've got to get out of here. I'm leaving."

"Where are you going?" he asked.

I replied, "I don't know, but if I don't get out of here now I am going to say or do something I will regret later. I can't handle any more of this right now."

I stormed out of the house without any clue of where I was going. The first thought that ran through my mind was to go to a bar to get drunk. I reasoned, *I've earned the right to get really drunk.*

As I pulled the car out of the driveway, pity fueled my rationalization that it was okay to go to the bar. But once I reached the outskirts of town, I realized I really did not want to get drunk. I asked myself, *What good would that do?* I had only been drunk one other time in my life, and I definitely did not like the experience. Suddenly getting drunk seemed like a stupid idea, but I still wanted to do something to ease the tension I felt. I wanted to lash out at someone else and make them hurt as badly as I did. As that thought entered my mind, I asked myself, "Is that why Heather lashes out, because the pain inside is so bad?"

I changed direction and headed to my church. I pulled into

the driveway and sat there in the car. After a few minutes, I went inside and kneeled at one of the pews. I fixed my gaze at the crucifix extended from the ceiling. As I looked at the crucifix, I thought of Jesus' pain and the suffering he went through, and I remembered how he lovingly suffered for us.

Soon, I felt foolish about my self-pity. I allowed my heart to open up, and I began to pray and let God's generous love and comfort console me.

I stayed at the church for another hour. As I drove home, I felt much better. Steve was waiting for me when I pulled into the driveway. I entered the house. He did not say anything to me. He just held his arms out, and I sunk deep into his chest. I stayed there a long time, his strong arms providing the love and comfort I needed so badly.

To this day, I don't think I could have handled Heather's illness by myself. Steve, my husband and friend, has always been my rock.

Steve and I dated for almost two years. Midway into our second year, I had completed my associate of arts degree in data processing but could not find suitable work in the town where we lived. When I was offered a good job as a programmer in a larger metropolitan city about three hours away, I accepted it. The decision was a difficult one; I was concerned it might mean the end of our relationship. Because we had not discussed marriage yet, I took advantage of the opportunity given to me and moved away to begin my new job.

Steve and I talked almost every night and saw each other on weekends. We dated long distance for about three months; then one weeknight around seven o'clock, my doorbell rang. Steve was standing at the door. I asked him what he was doing in town and he said, "I've been looking for a job all day."

This shocked me even more. "Why?" I asked.

He said, "We should be together—we should be married."

My hand tightened around the doorknob to steady myself. After what seemed like an eternity, I invited him in. I looked into his eyes, and my heart melted.

We were married four months later. Six months after our wedding Steve joined the air force. His family was shocked to hear he had joined the military. His parents remembered him saying as a teen that he would never go into the military. As a matter of fact, he did not even tell his parents about his decision until after he had enlisted. His mother did not believe him. I was the one who had to assure her it was true. His mother often found it difficult to discern fact from fiction with Steve.

To understand why, you have to understand the nature of the man I married. He has a great sense of humor. I think it is one of the reasons why we are still married.

Throughout our marriage, Steve's upbeat personality has helped me to lighten up when I could not handle the gravity of a situation. I'm sure he had to develop this trait as the last of eight children. He was also known through his school years as the class clown. Although I'm sure it challenged his parents' patience at times, he worked hard on the farm and was serious when the situation demanded it.

I remember him telling me the story of the time he was in college and awoke late one night with a terrible pain in his right side. It was so bad he got out of bed, bundled up, and went to the local drugstore for pain relievers. The medicine seemed to help for a little while, but soon the pain returned with a vengeance. He called his mother, a nurse, to ask what to do to relieve it. She responded by telling him to quit joking and let her go back to sleep. He tried to go back to sleep, but the pain was becoming unbearable, so he decided to go to the emergency room. As he waited, he called his mother again to let her know where he was and she again told him to stop playing around. It was not until after his surgery to remove an inflamed appendix that, when he called his mother for the third time, she finally believed him.

From then on, he learned to curb his joking. Fortunately for me, though, he did not lose enough of it to become a stick-in-the-mud. His strength and sense of humor have enabled me to hang in there during the worst times of dealing with Heather's illness.

Since the day program was on the way to work, I usually dropped Heather off in the morning. She used the drive time to angrily remind me of her displeasure with the program—blaming me for her being there. Some days it was all I could do to listen to her verbal assaults. By the time I dropped her off, the rest of the ride to work was my time alone to release. I often wept bitterly while trying to keep the car on the road; some mornings I had to pull over because I was so distraught.

When I arrived at work, I would sit in the car for a while to refresh my makeup and compose myself. The first few minutes in the building were the toughest. The usual greetings were hard as I gave my frozen smile while inside I was screaming.

Whenever someone asked me, "How are you today?" I wanted to shout, "I hurt like hell!" But, instead, I responded in a cursory, "I'm fine." As this game of denial became a safe haven, I soon became very clever at hiding my true feelings. In the long run, this made my healing more difficult because I eventually built up such a wall of denial that its numbness became second nature. To heal, I had to tear down that wall and feel the pain that allows recovery to begin.

Many nights I would sneak into Heather's bedroom and watch her sleep. As she lay sleeping, she looked so calm and peaceful, such a stark contrast from the reality of her daily struggles. During these quiet moments I allowed myself to dream of what her life could be without the pain she experienced. I asked God, *Please take her pain away and let her know you are there.*

February 8, 1996

Heather and I rarely talk anymore. Most times I don't even want to initiate contact with her. I never know how she is going to react. When she gets angry and yells at me, she just walks away afterward, ignoring me as if nothing happened. This is not the mother-daughter relationship I dreamed of. I want her touch. I long for her to wrap her arms around me and say, "I love you, Mom."

It was the end of February, and the temperature outside was below zero. Heather and I, along with Michael, were the only ones home. Heather and I got into an argument, and she cursed at me, "You bitch, I wish you were dead!"

I felt like a knife had been stuck in my chest and I froze in my tracks.

Then thinking, *How dare she speak to me like that,* I squared my shoulders and responded, "I'm your mother. You can't talk to me like that!"

Although that comment may have made a difference in another context, I quickly learned it was the wrong thing to say. All I did was open the door for Heather to verbally attack again, and attack she did. "Yeah, what are you going to do about it?"

Hurt and frustrated, I turned around and retreated to my bedroom, threw myself on the bed and buried my face into the pillow to drown out the sounds of my cries. It was utterly frustrating to deal with the myriad emotions that seized me during Heather's defiance.

I felt inadequate as a parent to "control" my daughter's behavior. I could not help but be hurt by her comments. And I felt like a prisoner in my own home, kept so by my own daughter, with no option save to merely put up with this every day. Retreating to my room was one of the ways I would isolate myself from her so I would not respond in kind.

Michael overheard this from his bedroom. He went into Heather's room and sternly told her not to talk to me that way. Then he came into my room and asked me, "Mom, are you all right?"

I responded, "I'll be okay in a few minutes."

He asked, "Do you want to talk about it?"

I was so touched by his compassion and surprised by his maturity but I, again, responded that I would be all right.

He persisted, "Are you sure you don't want to talk about it?"

I so desperately wanted to talk with someone, but I felt I could not talk to him. Instead, I told him, "I can't talk to you about it.

I don't want you to ever resent Heather or feel as if you have to take sides." He seemed to understand and left the room for me to deal with my feelings in private.

The next day Heather and I were home alone. After lunch, I asked her to wash the dishes. She was already in a surly mood, so I was not too surprised when she responded to me with a diatribe of expletives. I sent her to her room. Instead of obeying, she picked up one of the potted plants in the living room and smashed it against the wall—shattering the pot and spewing the freshly watered soil all over the furniture and carpet. I looked at her and could see by the harshness of her gaze and the firm set of her jaw that she was already in a rage. She then came at me with her fists, repeatedly striking me on the chest.

Although this had happened many times in the past, I had always been able to refrain from responding. But this time I blew it!

All my pent-up frustration and anger surfaced without any warning and came on with a vengeance. When Heather hit me again, I raised my right fist high in the air, ready to strike her—with all the force I could muster.

As my fist was behind my head, a flash of reason passed through my mind. Fortunately that was just enough time for me to rethink my actions, and I slowly lowered my fist. But that does not mean I was composed. Far from it!

I yelled at Heather, "Get out of here," as I pointed toward the front door. "You can't treat me like this. I don't have to live like this!" I repeated this several times as I paced around the room.

Fortunately, Heather did not respond by running out of the house, because I doubt that I would have gone after her. After a few minutes, I realized what I almost did, and I began trembling uncontrollably. I ran into my bedroom to try to calm down.

About an hour later, Steve came home. He immediately ran upstairs to our bedroom when he saw the condition of the house. After I described the incident to him, he encouraged me to stay in bed. I stayed there until the next morning, too upset to do anything else.

I had not realized how emotionally drained I was and it terrified me to think how close I had come to giving in to the rage.

February 27, 1996

Dear Heather,

I'm writing this letter to you even though I know I won't send it. But I have to put these words down on paper because if I don't I'm afraid I might act upon them. Just like I almost acted upon my own anger today.

I feel like I'm being controlled and manipulated by you. I feel like a hostage in my own house. I keep telling myself it's not you, but today I wanted to hurt you the way your behavior hurts me. A mother shouldn't hurt her daughter—she should heal her. What do I need to do to help you heal? I wish you would tell me. I wish you would talk to me. Maybe if we talked we could be closer but when I try to get close to you, you just push me away. What do you want from me? Please tell me!

One Saturday afternoon in March 1996, shortly after lunch, I was doing the dishes. The kids were in their rooms doing their homework. As I finished in the kitchen, I heard a commotion upstairs. I ran up the steps and noticed Heather yelling at Steve. Steve had checked in on Heather to find that she was not doing her homework. When he reminded her that it needed to be completed, she responded by yelling and cursing at him. Steve told her to go to her time-out room, but she refused.

Instead she picked up the glass of water on the nightstand and threw it against the wall. Then she began kicking the wall. She repeatedly kicked the wall—her rage increasing with each kick.

Then she bolted out of her room and toward the stairs. As she ran down the stairs, she said, "I'm going to kill myself by drowning in the lake." Heather ran through the door, heading straight toward the lake. Steve caught up with her about three houses down the street. In Heather's fits of mania she has tremendous strength, so in order to restrain her, Steve had to manhandle her.

Heather fought against his efforts, yelling as loud as she could, "I'm going to kill myself and you can't stop me."

This was happening outside in broad daylight for everyone to hear and see. One neighbor, who was standing outside, stared at Steve with a questioning look that asked if he was abusing her.

When Steve got Heather into the house, she was still very combative. Efforts to restrain Heather are not easy. In a rage she will attack anyone or anything in her way. I had a flower arrangement on the table with a glass vase. Heather picked up the vase and hurled it across the room, causing the glass to shatter all over the place. Just then, Heather escaped from Steve's grip and ran in the direction of the broken glass. Steve grabbed Heather by the legs in order to keep her from seriously injuring herself from the shards of glass.

She landed on the ground, hitting her chin with a thud. As they wrestled, Steve struggled to keep her safe while Heather kicked and screamed.

During the ensuing struggle Steve yelled to me, "Leslie, get the car started." Since we usually called 911 I was shocked by Steve's command, but I quickly went to the garage and started the car. Steve then hauled Heather in the back of the vehicle. I drove while Steve rode in the back with Heather. He continued trying to calm her but the more he tried, the more combative she became.

As they struggled in the backseat, Heather grabbed a ballpoint pen lying on the seat and tried to stab herself in the neck. Steve grabbed it from her but his hand came close enough to her mouth that she bit him. With her unsuccessful attempt at stabbing her neck, Heather threatened, "Maybe I can't kill myself now but I will OD on my medicine or strangle myself tonight."

Fortunately the hospital was not more than five miles away. It was very difficult for me to drive with this going on in the backseat.

Once admitted to the emergency room, Heather was given her usual shot of Thorazine and admitted for inpatient treatment.

This marked Heather's sixth hospitalization in less than a year! I was now completely familiar with the inpatient routine and frankly, relieved that we would at least get a few days of respite from this dangerous and controlling behavior. Our lives had spiraled into such a black hole of despair that soon bitterness and anguish made up the pattern of our everyday lives while I desperately fought to hold on to my faith that we would, somehow, get through this.

Heather was in the hospital for six days. This hospitalization resulted in maxing out our mental-health inpatient benefits. This meant we could no longer use inpatient hospitalization as a treatment option.

Unfortunately there exists a major discrepancy between medical and mental-health insurance benefits. The annual and lifetime limits for mental-health benefits are far less than for medical. Not knowing what we were dealing with was a big enough burden, but now being faced with this obstacle only made me feel like we were sinking further into the darkness. Because we could no longer use inpatient hospitalization, our only option during a psychiatric crisis was outpatient emergency treatment.

On Heather's last day in the hospital, Steve and I met with Dr. Johns to discuss a home treatment plan for her. During this discussion, Dr. Johns told us he felt Heather needed residential treatment. Just as Dr. Quinlen had suggested, Dr. Johns felt Heather needed extensive, round-the-clock treatment. But Dr. Johns prefaced that, "She needs treatment for just a little while—maybe six to nine months." My heart ached to hear this again, but I was beginning to realize he was probably right.

As Dr. Johns described the different treatment centers in the area I wrote down every word he said in order to do my own investigating to find the best place for Heather. Then he, like Dr. Quinlen, told us that Heather would have to be made a ward of the state. I jumped from the chair and cried, "A ward of the state? Why?"

Dr. Johns responded, "You need the state to pay for treatment, and in order to do so they require the state to be the legal ward of the child as a condition for accessing services."

I insisted, "I will not do that! There's no way I'm going to give up custody of Heather." The shrillness in my voice was evident when I asked, "Why would the state ask loving, caring parents to do such a thing? Aren't there other options?"

Dr. Johns said, "I know this is not what you two had in mind, but Heather is not getting any better at home, and I don't think she will with the kind of support the day program can provide. She needs intensive round-the-clock treatment. I know you don't like this option but I highly recommend you seek state ward through a no-fault custody."

Steve interrupted Dr. Johns to ask, "What do you mean by no-fault custody?"

Dr. Johns said, "I'm not a lawyer, and if you don't have one, I recommend you get one, but no-fault means that through no fault of your own you cannot provide adequate care to treat Heather's mental health prognosis."

He went on to say, "I am seriously concerned for the safety of Heather and your family. I highly recommend this avenue. As a matter of fact, if you choose not to, I have the authority to sub-poena the juvenile court for state placement on behalf of Heather, my patient. But I recommend that you initiate the action."

I could not believe what I was hearing. As I sat there, I wished I could wake up and find that this decision we had to make was just one big nightmare. We asked Dr. Johns for more time. He agreed, but prefaced it by saying; "If at any time I feel the situation is immi-nent I will petition the state for custody of Heather for residential treatment."

We left Dr. Johns's office in a daze. The mere thought of having to put our trust in the state's child protective services sent me into a panic.

Giving Up Custody of My Little Girl

We made it through the rest of March with only minor episodes from Heather. At this point, the only option for treatment when she became out of control was to take her to the emergency room where the doctor gave her a shot of Thorazine. After she fell into a drug-induced sleep, we took her home, and she slept for the rest of the night. I hated this method of treatment. I even remarked to Dr. Johns, "Dogs are treated better than this."

We tried to maintain a "normal" family life, but it was becoming harder each day. One early April day, Steve's employer had a company picnic. We were all suffering from cabin fever, so Steve and I, against our better judgment, decided to go. We all packed up the van and headed out early. Shortly after we began the trip, Heather and Mark started arguing. I tried to stop them, but just as I turned my back, Heather kicked Mark full force in the back, so hard that he lost his breath.

He was gasping for air. Heather just sat there watching him. I tended to Mark, and once I realized he would be okay, I turned to look at Heather but she just stared out the window. She did not even acknowledge what she had done. Steve and I decided to return home. Once at home, Heather was sent to her room, but she became even more defiant—refusing to go. Held captive once again by Heather's behavior, I felt very resentful and retreated to my bedroom for the rest of the day.

As things got worse at home, I often turned to my faith and fellow Christians for support. Many were very helpful and supportive, but I received my share of criticism also. More than once it was suggested to me and Steve that perhaps we were not "Christian enough" or that Heather's illness was because God was punishing us for our sins. Their underlying suggestion was that we would not struggle if we were really Christians.

At times like this I felt so alone, but I learned to turn to the Bible and prayer to get me through these hurtful comments. One especially comforting reading comes from John 9:3: "Neither this man nor his parents sinned," said Jesus, "but this happened so that the work of God might be displayed in his life."

The Bible clearly teaches that illness and maladies are not always the result of anyone's sin; they happen so the work of God can be manifested in a person's life. This passage helped me realize that God is more interested in my faithfulness and maturity in the face of suffering than He is in preventing me from experiencing pain.

These readings were important to me through my times of anger and resentment. I questioned God many times, asking, *Why me? Why my daughter?* In time I realized it was okay to get angry with God and question his ways. Questioning his ways brought me closer to him.

I do not always understand God's plan for us, and frankly, I do not like having to deal with Heather's illness, but I get solace from Paul in the book of 2 Corinthians where he prayed three times for the removal of affliction, and God's response to him was: "My grace is sufficient for thee" (12:9).

I know God made Heather just the way she is for a reason. I do not understand why Heather must struggle with this illness, but I continue to give God my faith and he gives me his grace.

One Saturday afternoon, Heather was edgy and irritable. She began arguing with me about something trivial, but fortunately she did not get out of control. When she calmed down, she went to her room to rest. She was unusually quiet as she lay on her bed.

I peered into her room and asked, "May I come in?"

I was surprised when she responded, "Yeah, come lie with me."

As I cuddled with her and wiped the tears from her cheeks, she asked me, "Why does God let me act like this? I don't want to be like this."

My heart was heavy with the weight of her question. I stroked her cheek and said, "Heather, I wish I had the answer, but I honestly don't know."

She searched my eyes for an answer and the tears flowed even more. I continued, "I know it's hard for us to understand God's ways, but please know he is there for you. I believe God has a plan for you. You are a special person and your struggling will not be in vain. We love you so much, so please don't give up."

I held on to her while she cried for a little longer. As she cried I pleaded, *God, she is tired and scared; please let her know you are there.*

As Steve and I began to realize that we could not provide the kind of care that Heather needed, I tried to prepare her for the possibility of out-of-home treatment. I told her, "Heather, we will do everything we can to help you, but in order to do that, that may mean you won't be able to live with us for a while."

She asked, "What do you mean?"

I said, "Heather, we have to find out what it is that is making you behave so extremely. That may mean you have to go to a place that can keep you safe when you get angry and can help you learn how to manage your moods. After that, you can come back home."

She asked, "For how long?"

I responded, "Hopefully not too long, but we have to do something soon to help you."

With this response she became quiet and laid her head in my arms. Eventually she fell asleep. I lay there holding her until my arm went numb under the weight of her head.

I went into the living room to read. Heather awoke an hour later and came downstairs with a pillow and suitcase in her hand. When our eyes met, she said to me, "Mom, I've got to leave before I make you hate me."

Immediately the tears welled up in my eyes and I said, "Heather, I could never hate you."

I don't know what made her believe she needed to leave, but I knew she was serious so I couldn't ignore her statement.

I said, "Heather, if you ever need to leave, I will find a safe place for you to go, but please don't run away and make me and Dad worry if you are safe."

I then asked her, "But will you stay here for now?"

She nodded in agreement and put her stuff back in her bedroom.

March 9, 1996

Dear God,
I told Heather today that you have a plan.
I sure wish I knew what that plan was. I
would hate to think that I was lying to her.
Are you there? Do you hear me?

Getting through each day was becoming increasingly challenging. Although I voiced the words to Heather in preparation of out-of-home placement, I still struggled to accept this option. But it was becoming harder to ignore the fact that we could not provide the kind of care Heather needed.

Dr. Johns knew of our reluctance to use this option, but finally, with his urging, Steve and I began to research the various treatment centers in our community.

The greatest fear about this decision is that it meant we had to give up legal custody of Heather. I could not understand why parents would be forced to make such a decision in order to get the treatment needed for their child. This decision tore at the very core of my fears and guilt.

I called Ms. Calkin for legal guidance. She had helped us for previous matters, but she was completely unsupportive in our option for state ward. She said to me, "You are making a grave mistake. You can never trust Child Protective Services and the juvenile court system."

Her comments shook me. After speaking with Ms. Calkin, I was confused and began to doubt our decision. I called Steve at work and asked him to meet me for lunch. Just two days prior, we agreed on the decision to seek the state's help even though it meant giving up custody temporarily, but Ms. Calkin's comments gave me serious pause.

Steve and I met in the park on a beautiful, sunny, spring day but my outlook did not match the beauty of the day. I described Ms. Calkin's comments to Steve and he, too, began to have the same doubts and reconsidered our decision. Even though we knew our options were limited, we decided we would try to hold on longer, hoping for this to turn around—and quickly!

We could not stand the thought of having to give up legal custody of Heather. It was not right. What Steve and I feared the most was that once Heather was placed in the hands of a state bureaucratic system, our parental rights would be eliminated or severely restricted. Having heard several horror stories of loving parents being wrongly accused, by the state's court system, of gross injustices against their children haunted me.

We naively thought that rather than placing Heather into the legal hands of the state we could find a treatment center and pay for it ourselves.

Another month went by and all this did was buy precious little time. Heather's aggressive behavior continued to escalate. I was always on pins and needles, and the boys spent most of the time in their rooms, away from Heather. My family was coming apart. I felt hopeless to know how to mend it.

In desperation, I took a day off from work and called all the state agencies trying to get as much information as possible regarding treatment for children with behavior problems like Heather's.

Because Steve and I had some equity built in our house we thought we could borrow against it and pay for treatment ourselves. We thought it could not cost any more than one to two thousand dollars a month. Although this would cause greater financial hardship, we were willing to do it if it meant Heather would not have to be made a ward of the state.

When I spoke with the director of two group homes in the area I was shocked to hear of the expense. It was more like a thousand dollars a day! My hopes were sinking fast. I made another call to a group home and spoke with a case worker from the Child Protective Services division.

I described Heather's behavior pattern and abuses toward myself and her younger brother and the danger she posed to herself. When I finished, he said, "Mrs. Byers, I know you are genuinely concerned about your daughter, but you are just as responsible for the safety of your other children, and it appears to me they are in just as much danger as Heather."

This startled me! Steve and I had been so consumed with worry and fear for Heather that we, unconsciously and irrationally, had lost sight of the risk to the boys. It suddenly became painfully obvious that Steve and I were not thinking very clearly. We realized we had to turn to the state in order to get the right treatment for Heather.

The next day Steve and I shared this decision with Dr. Johns. He had been patiently waiting for us to agree to this and I could sense he was not willing to wait much longer. With this decision, he immediately moved forward with efforts to initiate the petition for state assistance for Heather.

On April 23, 1996, Dr. Johns sent an affidavit to the District Attorney for the Juvenile Court, Child Protective Services division, requesting state assistance for placement into a residential treatment center.

Once the affidavit was sent, things began happening fast. Steve and I realized that we needed to get another lawyer. We did not understand the juvenile court system and all its rules and procedures, but mostly we wanted the court attorneys to realize that Steve and I were not neglectful or abusive to our children. We had already experienced so much parent bashing and accusations by professionals that we were concerned the courts might perceive Heather's problems to be the result of child neglect or abuse.

We found a lawyer, Juanita Adams, who had assisted other parents through the juvenile court system. During discussions with Ms. Adams, we learned more about the no-fault category for state custody. No fault states that the child cannot receive the appropriate care and supervision relative to her developmental needs, through no fault of the parents. Even with the no-fault petition, Steve and I were fearful the state's attorney would presume incompetence on our part and terminate our parental rights.

Ms. Adam's primary job was to make sure our rights remained intact and that Steve and I continued to be a part of the decisions made during the course of Heather's treatment, with the ultimate goal of getting her back into our home as quickly as possible.

April 24, 1996

Today Steve and I made the most agonizing decision. We put Heather into the hands of the state. I feel like I'm being boxed into a corner. My God, why should any parent have to make this decision? I hope she does not hate us for this.

A week later, on May 2, 1996, I was called to the lobby at work. When I arrived, I was handed a summons to appear in court in regards to the petition for state ward placement for Heather. I had never set foot in a courtroom before; this formal process of being summoned made me feel like a criminal. I quickly realized that this was a serious legal proceeding and was glad Steve and I had had the foresight to hire a lawyer to lead us through the process.

The court appearance was held on May 14, 1996. I remember the day as clearly as if it were yesterday. Although Steve and I knew we had run out of options, I still struggled with a peaceful conclusion to this decision. Steve and I sat at a table with our lawyer while the array of state attorneys and staff sat across from us. I was not prepared for how formidable the atmosphere was.

Ms. Adams could sense my discomfort and she tried to explain what to expect, but she was cut off midsentence when the judge entered the room and the bailiff commanded, "All rise!"

Without any introduction the judge immediately began the proceedings. The attorney for the state read the court petition seeking custody of Heather. My insides felt tight and a solid lump was caught in my throat. The attorney continued to read the petition describing the history of Heather's deteriorating mental-health. The judge spoke with the state's attorneys for clarification on the petition and then turned toward Steve and me. When our eyes met, I froze in terror. The judge explained the process of placing Heather in the hands of the state Child Protective Service and juvenile court system. He then said, in a terse formal tone, that, at the moment, he saw no need to terminate our parental rights but emphasized that, if at any time, we jeopardized Heather's treatment, our parental rights would immediately be terminated.

I began to feel like I was the one on trial. This did nothing to assuage my fears, but a reassuring glance from Ms. Adams enabled me to remain calm through the rest of the proceedings.

The hearing took less than ten minutes. At the conclusion, Steve and I were no longer the legal guardians of Heather. When the judge pounded his gavel to end the proceedings, I felt sick and hollow inside. I was consumed with doubt about the decision and wanted to take it back.

Ms. Adams, sensing my anxiety, tried to assure me that it would be okay, but she could not stay any longer because she had to meet with the state's attorney. I turned toward Steve and I could see by the deepening crease in his forehead that he was upset, too.

He reached out to me and we held each other for a few minutes. Neither of us said anything, but each of us was aware of the pain the other was feeling. I could not maintain my composure any longer. I went into the restroom and sat in the stall, sobbing. I must have been in there for thirty minutes. Once the tears dried, I went to Ms. Adams to find out where Heather would be placed.

Heather was appointed a case worker, Emily Wallace, and a guardian ad litem, Annie Giles. Ms. Wallace represented the state and Ms. Giles represented Heather, independently from all other parties. It was Ms. Wallace and Ms. Giles's responsibility to assess Heather's level of placement needs and recommend a treatment plan to the district attorney for the juvenile courts. Placement services range from the least restrictive environment (a therapeutic foster home) to the most restrictive environment (a residential treatment center). During the discussions Ms. Wallace and Ms. Giles had with Heather, it became apparent to them that Heather's anger and suicidal ideations were a constant struggle for her.

It was quickly concluded that Heather's case was serious enough to warrant placement in a residential treatment center. I was relieved to hear this. This option meant Heather would be safe and receive the kind of therapy and intense mental-health attention she needed until proper diagnosis and treatment were found.

I was afraid a foster or group home could not provide that level of security. In the case of Child Protective Services, their goal, like the school system's, is to place a ward in the least restrictive environment that will match the child's needs. I felt putting Heather in the wrong place would only prolong the goal of diagnosis and recovery, or worse yet, deteriorate her situation.

A foster home is the first level of out-of-home placement. I was so concerned that Heather was simply going from our home, a loving, caring environment where her parents and siblings knew her, to a foster home that was filled with many other troubled children. Fortunately this did not happen.

The state's escalation to a more restrictive environment was a sign that they really understood the severity of Heather's problem. But, at the time, there were no openings in any of the local facilities. So, while we waited for an opening, Heather continued to live in our home, even though she was legally a ward of the state.

After the court hearing, I was still too upset to go back to work so I went home. Because Steve was a contractor, if he didn't work he did not get paid, so he went back to work. The legal and medical bills were mounting and Ms. Adams had warned us earlier that the state would probably come after us for monthly child support.

Since we weren't sure yet how much that was going to cost, we needed every penny we could get. I was glad Steve went back to work because I just wanted to be by myself. Once I got home, I tried to keep busy, but I could not concentrate on anything so I curled up in my bed and tried to read. Instead I cried for a long time.

Finally I sat up in bed and began to pray. At first my prayers were more like angry accusations at God: *God, why would you allow this to happen to our family? Why won't you help us?*

Suddenly my mother's past advice about my aunt Suzie's struggles with bipolar came back to me. I wished I had thought back then to ask my mother about it more, but she was gone now, and I did not know whom to turn to. I decided to call my mother's sister, Mary Jane, in the hopes that she might have some information about Suzie's illness. I explained the circumstances with Heather, and I asked her, "What was Suzie like as a child?"

Mary Jane surprised me by saying, "You know, if you call Suzie, she will talk to you."

I was not expecting this response. I thought talking with

Suzie out of the blue about her illness might be uncomfortable for her, but I desperately needed to talk to someone else who struggled with mental-health problems.

Mary Jane called Suzie and within ten minutes Suzie called me. The conversation was awkward at first, but as I described Heather's behavior Suzie said something that stuck with me.

She said, "Mania is terrible. You have to get it under control before Heather can begin to learn how to live with this illness. You cannot reach the person in the manic state." She said with great emotion, "It is too violent—the rage is all-consuming. It's rare that anyone goes for help during a manic episode. During mania, the person is beyond reasoning and logic. They don't think they need any help. They think everyone else is being unreasonable. It's the depression that saves us, because it is so painful we will do anything to make it stop."

We talked for only a few more minutes, but I felt a strange sense of calmness.

Suzie, while struggling with mental illness as a young adult, had learned to manage her life with bipolar. Today she lives a successful, healthy, happy life as a nurse, mother, and grandmother. Her triumphs helped me realize that Heather, too, could overcome her illness.

I went back into my room and began to pray again with more intensity than I have ever prayed in my life. First I bargained with God, telling him, *I will do anything, if only you will heal my little girl.* I continued bargaining, sure that I could think of a way to fix Heather. Then suddenly I stopped praying. I realized I was trying to tell God how to fix the problem rather than letting go of my burden and really giving it to him. I just kept getting in the way.

Steve once said to me, "Leslie, one of the greatest things I like about you—your strength and ability—is also one of the greatest challenges to live with. You are so capable that many times you don't allow others to help you."

At that moment, I knew I was doing the same thing with accepting help, both from God and the state. As I sat in bed, I released the burden to God and let go of the years of fear and anguish that had become a part of my daily struggle. I decided I was not going to give in to fear and hopelessness. In that space where fear once lived, a sense of peace and calm entered.

As the weight of anxiety lifted from my heart, I felt God saying to me, "Leslie, how I long for you to understand. What happens is not dependent upon what you can or can't do. I will make the difference, if you let me."

I felt calmer at that moment than I had in years. It was such a feeling of surrender—total and complete. I still did not know when or how God would handle this, I just knew he would give our family the strength we needed when we needed it.

The next week, Friday, May 28, 1996, Heather became out of control and began attacking Mark. I had to call 911 for help. A sheriff was dispatched and arrived within ten minutes. When the sheriff came into the house and saw how combative Heather was, he had to handcuff her. He put Heather in the squad car and took her to the emergency room—where she was treated with Thorazine and released.

Because Heather was now a ward of the state, I had to call Ms. Wallace to let her know of the incident. As Emily and I talked on the phone, she asked to speak with Heather.

I told her, "You can't. She is knocked out and will be for the rest of the night."

Ms. Wallace said, "That's not acceptable. I'm coming over." When she arrived she went immediately to Heather's room. Ms. Wallace tried to awaken Heather by gently shaking her, but Heather could only utter a groan. She could not even lift her head off the pillow or open her eyes.

I said to Emily, "This is the only treatment option we have left, and this happens most nights. The way Heather is being treated is inhumane. We have no more inpatient medical benefits through our health insurance, and Dr. Johns will not try Heather on medications for bipolar."

Ms. Wallace placed a call to Dr. Johns. Once she had him on

the phone she said, "This is Emily Wallace, case worker for Heather Byers. I am ordering Heather to be placed in the hospital for a minimum of forty-eight hours for a medication evaluation. I want Heather taken off Thorazine and put on the appropriate medication to treat bipolar."

I couldn't believe what I was hearing! Emily, too, realized that Heather's current method of treatment was not right.

Heather spent Memorial Day weekend in the hospital for the medication evaluation and, as per Ms. Wallace's insistence, Dr. Johns changed Heather's medication from Thorazine to Lithium. Finally, they were trying something for bipolar!

The hospital stay was relatively short compared to the others, only two and a half days. As a result of being taken off of Thorazine, Heather was much more alert and active. I was glad to see her released from the dulling effects of the Thorazine.

Heather came home on Monday, June 1, but only for a very short time. On June 5, 1996, Heather was removed from our home and put in the residential treatment center.

Part Five:
Coming Out of the Darkness

Treatment and Safety

The residential treatment center (RTC) is referred to as a lockdown facility. All doors are on electronic locks. Parents and visitors have to be escorted through the building at all times. Visits have to be arranged with the staff. The children in the treatment center are referred to as residents. They range in age from nine to fourteen. In the event a child becomes combative or threatening, crisis alarms sound and policemen and security guards are summoned. During a crisis (when a resident becomes combative or out of control) all residents not involved have to be in their rooms. It is a formidable atmosphere—much like a prison.

I visited Heather the next day—after I called to get permission. Having to get permission to see my daughter was difficult for me to accept at first.

I soon learned that treatment for a behavior disorder involves a combination of medications and psychotherapy. Many mental illnesses are a result of a chemical imbalance in the brain and are effectively treated with proper medications and therapy. Medications alone are not the most effective treatment program. Medications moderate the illness and make psychotherapy possible. Psychotherapy heals and teaches the patient and their loved ones how to live with the illness.

There are two types of psychotherapy—behavioral and cognitive therapy. Behavioral therapy helped Heather to gain control of her impulsive behaviors. Cognitive therapy allows her to manage her thought processes by helping her to assess situations realistically and to develop ways to change her behavior before it gets out of control.

The combination of medications and psychotherapy provides a powerful tool in managing mental illness. One component without the other lessens the effectiveness and timeliness of the patient's recovery. I eventually learned how important it was for Heather's treatment and healing that we understood the therapeutic components of the program at the residential treatment center, so we could be a part of her recovery rather than impeding it.

Our first visit did not go well. We were seated in a room shared by others. I moved to the corner, away from the other residents to give us some semblance of privacy. When Heather entered the room she held a defiant gaze at me. I reached out to her but she immediately retorted, "Why did you give me away?"

The previous evening, when Heather had met with one of the staff, she learned that she was a legal ward of the state. Heather thought we abandoned her. The mere thought of the anguish she experienced as she lay in a bed all night, thinking we gave her away, tore at my heart.

I tried to explain the situation, "Heather, we didn't give you away. You are our daughter and you always will be."

She said, "They told me the state is my legal guardian."

I was so angry that Heather found this out this way. When I spoke with Emily the day Heather was made a ward of the state, I asked her not to say anything to Heather.

Steve and I wanted to tell Heather, instead of her learning it from someone else. There was never the right opportunity. Heather was constantly out of control. And I did not think she would be placed in the treatment center so soon.

I had come that morning to the RTC to tell Heather the truth. But it was too late. I said to her, "Heather, we had no other choice. This was the only way we could get help."

She retorted, "I hate you! I hate you! You don't even care about me!"

My voice trembled as I said, "Heather, I care enough about you to not care what you think about me right now. If helping you to become a whole person means you hate me, than I accept that. I hope you will realize someday that Dad and I did this because we love you and we will never give up on you."

She didn't move. She just stared at me. I stood frozen in place; vacillating between wanting to hold her and thinking I should probably let her deal with her emotions on her own terms. Eventually I gave in and pulled her to me. Soon her anger melted, and she enveloped me and wept quietly in my chest. She said to me, "I don't want to live here."

I lifted her face, wiped the tears from her eyes and with conviction in my voice said, "Heather, you will be with your family again soon—I know it. We want you back home, but we can't let this illness control our lives anymore. We will always be here for you. And when you beat this thing, you will come back home."

We talked for a few more minutes and then Heather had to go to the group-therapy session. As we said our good-byes, Heather turned to look at me. I noticed a slight smile appear at the corner of her mouth. It was not much, but I hung on to the memory of that smile to help get me through the loneliness of her absence.

The first few weeks of Heather's absence were hard. I constantly thought of her and worried that she was okay. With her absence, the house was suddenly quiet—almost too quiet. Because our family had dealt with the disruption of Heather's behavior for so long, its effects became a "normal" pattern of life. It wasn't until after the second week that my family began to go on more outings. Nothing fancy or elaborate—just family road trips to the zoo, the museum, or the movies, some planned and many spontaneous.

After one such outing, it dawned on me just how isolated we had been as a result of Heather's illness. I could not remember the last time our family had gone out together.

The first holiday without Heather, July 4, was a difficult time for me. Our family, along with two of Steve's sisters and their families, was invited to visit his sister Katy in Minnesota for the long weekend. I was torn between staying home and going to Minnesota. Going meant that Heather would spend the weekend without any visits from her family. Also, I did not think I could handle a visit with Steve's family. They knew of Heather's placement only from a brief conversation between Steve and Katy, but other than that, nothing else had been said. I could not talk about Heather because each time I tried, I could only get a few words out before the tears overcame me.

Steve and I were undecided even up until the day we were scheduled to leave. That morning I received a call from the nurse at the RTC and was told that Heather would not be allowed any visitors for the weekend because she was too combative. Heather was still having a hard time accepting her stay at the RTC and seemed to be lashing out at everyone.

In light of the situation, we decided to go to Minnesota.

Katy loves to cook and entertain. She and her family live on a farm in the country. The kids enjoy the wide open spaces of the farm. The trip there was uneventful but with each mile closer to Katy's, the more the ache I felt for Heather gnawed at me. I didn't want to spoil the trip for the others, so I put on my happy face.

The next day, all the men were outside and the women, three of my sister-in-laws and I, sat at the kitchen table drinking coffee and talking. Katy, who had lost her fifth and last child to an accident when he was seven, began to reminisce about him. Although it had been ten years since his death, she still talked about her son from time to time. As she reminisced, the tears welled up in my eyes, spilling over onto my cheeks. I was crying for my child as well as Katy's. I felt like I had lost Heather to the ravages of her anger.

On the evening of July 4, the kids were anxious to set off their fireworks. When it became dark we all gathered outside. The kids launched fireworks as the adults sat on the porch watching. I know how Heather loves fireworks. I hated it that she could not be with us to celebrate. I could not stop thinking about her. I wanted her to be with us so badly.

Steve was carrying on a lively conversation with his family, so I took a moment to sneak around the side of the house to be alone. It was then that I let out my cries of anguish. Before long, I was sobbing so violently my body was wracked in pain. Fortunately, the fireworks drowned the sound.

July 13, 1996

Today I was in the mall and I noticed a mother and daughter sitting in the food court. The daughter was probably eleven or twelve years old. They looked like they had just finished shopping because the little girl was going through the bags, reviewing each outfit. I sat there in my chair just staring at them—watching them intently with an ache in my heart growing larger by the minute. The tears spilled onto my cheeks. Evidently they could feel my stares because they both turned to me. I wiped the tears from my eyes and turned away and thought, Why can't that be me and Heather?

When I think back to where Heather was placed, I realize how fortunate we were that she received treatment through the Boys Town (now Girls & Boys Town) RTC program. For years, Girls & Boys Town has successfully helped adolescents from all walks of life overcome their unique challenges. In addition, we were fortunate that Heather did not have to be placed in an institution in another state. The center was almost halfway between my home and work.

It was a ten minute drive from either direction. During the weekdays, I would periodically visit Heather for lunch, before, or after work, and on weekends I spent as many afternoons or evenings with her as were allowed.

Heather was assigned a therapist, Karen Galin, to help her develop better ways to deal with her extreme mood swings. Medication for bipolar helps to even out the severity of mood swings the patient experiences, stabilizing the behavior to a more manageable level. But with bipolar, the person develops a behavior pattern—I call it Heather's anger cycle—that becomes ingrained in the person's subconscious thought. When Heather gets in a manic state, she typically begins the foul language and then proceeds to slam doors or bang on walls; then she may pick up an object and throw it. She will continue to escalate this behavior until someone has to intervene.

Once during family therapy I asked Heather why she lets a little thing such as her displeasure over a meal escalate into a fullblown crisis.

She said, "I replay my frustration about something over and over in my mind until it becomes a catastrophe. I don't know how to let it go."

This statement helped me to understand the thinking patterns associated with bipolar. With this illness, Heather is robbed of the brain chemicals that regulate thoughts and moods. Through medication and therapy, Heather can focus on her thinking patterns and learn to change her negative thought processes to more positive responses.

A diabetic doesn't simply take insulin every day and ignore the importance of a balanced daily diet and periodic monitoring of his blood sugar level. The same is true for Heather. She has to take medications every day. She also has to monitor her mood barometer and consciously follow an anger-management plan when the mania or depression becomes overwhelming.

Because Heather was removed from our home due to her volatility and threat to me, it was Karen's role to work with Heather and us to ensure that Heather could manage her illness before she could return home. In addition to individual therapy for Heather, our family went through extensive family therapy. We all needed to understand this illness in order to provide a support system for Heather.

The therapy helped us to heal from the wounds built up over the years of living with this illness. For quite some time after Heather's threat against me, I struggled with how to feel about it. As her mother, I love her with all my heart. As a person, I was deeply hurt and confused by her words. I had to learn how to deal with my feelings about Heather's years of aggression towards me if we were to have a chance of a healthy mother-daughter relationship.

As Heather's parents, Steve and I had to balance the need to make her accountable for her actions while, at the same time, supporting and forgiving her. She was already beating herself up about her past behaviors. It would not help if we could not let go.

Around the second week of July, I began to see an improvement in Heather's demeanor. She seemed to be less tense and more animated. She even wore a smile once in a while. Her improvement was evident by the fact that by the middle of July, the good days were outweighing the bad. She had fewer explosive episodes each day and even spent a few days a week with no episodes of rage. Her outlook on life appeared to be more positive as she engaged in fun-loving interaction with others.

By the latter part of July, Heather hit a major milestone—she went two full weeks without any raging episodes. She seemed happier than I had seen her in several years. As a result of this improvement, Heather was given her first pass—a two-hour unsupervised leave with me.

It was a great feeling to have time alone with my little girl, to be her mother once again without constantly having someone look over us. Knowing the two hours would pass quickly, I asked Heather, "Where do you want to go?"

She immediately responded, "I want to go to Dairy Queen."

We both love Dairy Queen, and it was not too far from the RTC. As we ate our ice cream, we talked the entire time. Heather shared with me her hopes and dreams of getting out of the RTC and coming home. It was a wonderful visit with absolutely no tension between us.

I realized as I was driving back to the RTC that those two hours were the first time in a long while that we shared any real tenderness.

As Heather improved, she received more passes, each progressively longer, until she worked her way up to an overnight pass to come home. It was wonderful to have Heather back in our home even if it was only for one night.

By the first week of August, though, Heather reverted and was on edge all the time. By the second week of August she was plagued with feelings of aggression and suffered frequent outbursts again. I was completely frustrated by the turn of events and asked the treatment center doctor, Dr. Sims, for clues as to why Heather was reverting to her negative behavior.

He replied, "Well, I took her off the lithium a few weeks ago, so maybe that has something to do with it."

Agitated, I asked, "Why?"

He replied, "This is a serious medication to strap someone with, and if Heather really doesn't need it I don't want to continue it."

I admired his reason, but I could clearly see the positive effect this medication had on leveling Heather's moods. Because Heather was not taking any medications, other than what was given during a severe episode to calm her down, I asked him, "How much longer will you monitor the situation before you decide she needs to be put back on meds?"

Dr. Sims responded, "I will closely monitor her behavior pattern over the next five days, and if there isn't any improvement, I will put her back on the lithium."

Without any medications Heather became more combative and, true to his word, within five days she was back on the lithium.

Lithium takes a few weeks before it becomes effective. So by the first week of September, Heather had begun to improve again. The contrast with Heather's behavior and demeanor when properly treated versus her behavior when untreated was mind boggling to me. Untreated, Heather relapses into a roller coaster of moods so extreme that they torment her daily existence.

During the times of Heather's rage, her anger destroys her ability to feel the warmth of love and security of family and friends. Treated, Heather is a compassionate, intelligent, articulate, and fun-loving person.

During the month of September, Heather spent every weekend at home, reestablishing bonds with her family. As she continued to improve and spend more time at home, it became increasingly hard for her to remain patient. Heather really wanted to come home. Karen had to remind Heather that she had at least a couple more months of treatment.

The next day, when I visited Heather, she was melancholy. I asked her, "What's wrong?"

She replied, "Karen told me I have to be here at least a couple more months. I don't know if I can take this place much longer."

I was just as impatient as Heather was for her to come home, but I also wanted to make sure she used this time to cement her knowledge and strength for the challenges that lay ahead for her.

I said to her, "Heather, just take things one day at a time. That is the only way I am getting through this. And when your strength is gone, turn to God. He will be your strength for you."

She replied, "I know Mom, it's just so hard."

An Answer—At Last!

I did not know it at the time, but Dr. Sims decided to take Heather off lithium again. However, it did not take long for me to realize something was amiss.

Heather quickly reverted to her volatile behavior and surly demeanor. It was incredible to me that Dr. Sims would do such a thing again. But he emphasized, like the last time, he really wanted to be sure she needed the medication and did not use it as a crutch. I wanted to be angry with him, but I could not. He really wanted to be sure of Heather's diagnosis and treatment. Because there is no blood test for bipolar, the only way to be certain that this is, in fact, what she is afflicted with is to try the on-again, off-again test with medications and therapy.

Dr. Sims waited until the middle of October before placing Heather back on the lithium and within two weeks the cycle of recovery resumed. I was amazed at the way Heather positively responded to lithium. With medication, she is able to lead a very healthy, productive life.

Toward the beginning of November, during an update meeting with Heather's care team, Dr. Sims said, "Well, I believe I can say conclusively that Heather responds well to lithium." In five months she had been placed on and then off this medication three times. Each time the near-miraculous improvement associated with this medication is very conclusive."

Heather's progress was remarkable. She seemed so happy and content with life. The old surly face was replaced with one of ease and comfort. Heather now spent every weekend and one night a week at home.

During one evening in the latter part of October, Heather and I went down to the lake to enjoy the fall colors as the leaves turned their beautiful autumn hues. We sat by the lakeshore making plans for Heather's return home. Soon the sun began to set in the sky. Heather had brought along her camera and took several shots of the sun fading in the sky. Later, when I had the pictures developed, I was amazed to see a trio of pictures, in sequence, capturing the beauty of the setting sun against the backdrop of the lake. The pictures spoke of such great hope and renewal that I had them professionally matted into a collage and hung them in the living room. To this day they serve as a reminder of the beginning of the end of Heather's roulette wheel of rage that took us so deep into the darkness that, at times, I wondered if we could ever get out.

The second week in November, Steve and I met with Heather's case worker, doctor, and therapist. Without warning or introduction, Dr. Sims announced that Heather was ready to be released.

I was ecstatic yet cautious. Just a few months earlier, Heather was out of control most of the time and, in a near-constant manic state. We so badly wanted Heather home, but we were concerned it was too early. Steve said to Dr. Sims.

"Are you sure she's ready?"

Sensing our caution, Dr. Sims said, "Heather is responding very well to the medication. Because of this, she no longer meets the criteria for being here."

Medications are a huge part of the recovery, but we felt Heather needed more therapy. I did not want Heather's life to be like a yo-yo, in and out of treatment centers. But Dr. Sims assured us that Heather would continue to receive therapy and counseling once she returned home.

While I questioned whether Heather was ready to come home, the next day, during our visit, she shared with me a decision she had come to a week prior.

She told me, "Mom, I don't want to live like this anymore. I have to turn this around."

As she talked, she pounded her fist to her heart for emphasis and said, "I have to do this!"

This statement held so much hope! Until Heather was able to make this mature discovery and decide to beat this thing herself, Steve and I had to do all we could to keep her safe.

Heather further went on to say, "Mom, I know I have hurt you and Dad so much. You always forgave me. I think that is why I always lashed out at you, because I knew you would forgive me. But if I don't change, you might hate me."

With mixed emotions I was relieved to hear that Heather accepted her illness and was trying to reconcile with it. But, as a mother, it was hard to see my child suffer so before she realized the power of her will.

With this statement, I knew that Heather had begun to develop in maturity and strength. Accepting this illness and facing it head-on were the first critical steps to overcoming it.

The Monster Called Bipolar

Bipolar plays havoc with Heather's moods. It can vacillate rapidly between periods of extreme highs, or mania, to periods of extreme lows, or depression. She may experience these highs and lows—or a combination of both. It is in this combination, known as the mixed state where she experiences both highs and lows, that Heather is most irritable and violent. One patient has described this mixed state as, "feelings of being lost, empty, forlorn, and hopeless. These feelings, combined with the intense energy of mania, make me feel desperate, panicky, and threatened. Having all of these feelings intertwined is absolutely hellish."

This mixed state is what Heather exhibited most frequently, although she would periodically swing from manic to depressive. Another trait most common to the mixed state is extreme paranoia—an irrational fear that has no basis in fact and can be triggered by anything.

For example, one day at Heather's school, two girls were having a conversation at lunch—just a general conversation about things that girls talk about—when Heather approached them, and in a loud and demanding voice, asked them why they were talking about her. She repeatedly shouted to them, "Why are you talking about me? You have no right to talk about me!" Of course this scared the girls, but Heather would not stop until she was removed from the lunchroom.

Manic episodes usually develop rapidly, maybe over a course of days, or on occasion a few hours. But the onset is usually more rapid with each successive episode. The episodes, depending on the individual, can last three to six months, with some reported cases as long as one year. In the early manic stages, Heather will feel highly energetic and very positive, as if she can accomplish anything.

Dr. Kay Redfield Jamison, a professor of psychiatry at the Johns Hopkins School of Medicine, and a bipolar patient, describes this illness as "the only mental illness that has a good side." But that good side—the intense pleasurable energy and euphoria during mania—is usually short-lived because the mania cannot be tolerated for more than a few days.

In mania, Heather's thoughts will race. She may have many plans and ideas, although most of them may not get accomplished. Her speech becomes rapid. As the energy in the manic state becomes spent, her motor burns out, and she becomes increasingly irritable and easily agitated. Her behavior turns hostile and explosive.

Mania brews a dangerous combination of poor impulse control, poor judgment, irritability, and grandiosity. In mania, Heather engages in behaviors that are at odds with her normal character. Thoughts became fragmented, and she sometimes has delusions of grandeur or paranoia.

The manic highs and depressive lows of bipolar are neurobiological in origin, yet they manifest psychologically. The biochemical underpinnings of the thought and belief structures of the person with bipolar are so distorted that his or her thinking no longer works like everyone else's. This is why Heather may not accept the fact that a problem exists. She often reasons, "It's everyone else that has a problem."

Scientists believe bipolar is a chemical imbalance in the brain that results in the inability to control moods and thoughts. So in this sense, bipolar is not a mental illness (sickness of the mind), but a physical illness of the brain. That is why medical treatment, along with behavioral and psychotherapy, is so successful.

The success rate for treatment of bipolar is 80 percent or better. Today the major clinical problem in treating this illness is not that there is a lack of effective medications, but that patients often refuse to take them, primarily because of the stigma associated with having to admit they are taking medications for a mental disorder.

Doctors believe that heredity is a strong influencing factor in the development of this illness. Some studies indicate that bipolar is often, but not always, inherited from the mother's side of the family. This is important in Heather's case because there is a family history of bipolar that is directly connected to my mother's side of the family.

The symptoms of children with bipolar are often viewed as a behavior problem rather than a mood problem. Early diagnosis is critical; a delay may be devastating to the child and her family. Besides the obvious disruption to the child's life during the acute episodes, a child who is dealing with bipolar does not go through the normal developmental experiences in the same way that other children do because she is trying to keep her own thoughts and moods under control. She may end up with a developmental lag—months or years behind other children—when she emerges into her twenties.

Diagnosis before age ten was once uncommon. Although Heather was officially diagnosed in the summer of 1996, at the age of ten, hospital records referred to the possibility of this diagnosis as early as Heather's first hospitalization in 1995, at which time she was only eight years old.

The symptoms of children with bipolar are typically different from the symptoms of adult-onset bipolar for two reasons. A child under the age of twelve often first develops atypical depression symptoms, such as little need for sleep, and behavioral problems (including sudden, long-lasting temper outbursts). The child may break things or become combative. This was certainly true in Heather's episodes and was initially disguised as bad parenting by Steve and me, or in some instances, as a personality weakness on the part of Heather.

Another difference between child- and adult-onset bipolar is that up to the age of twelve, the episodes tend to be continuous rather than episodic. This combination of the extreme volatility, or rage, and the continuous nature of child-onset bipolar became the pattern of behavior Heather exhibited for many years, to the point that its consequences eventually became a "normal" way of life for us.

In addition, bipolar in children exhibits many of the same characteristics of a child suffering from Attention Deficit Hyperactivity Disorder (ADHD). In both disorders, the child may be irritable, impulsive, distractible, and hyperactive.

Misdiagnosis is a common problem with children suffering from bipolar. Heather's first diagnosis, ADHD, was treated with Ritalin, a stimulant. Ritalin had the effect of putting fuel to the fire—it increased Heather's aggression rather than lessening it.

Later, when she was prescribed Prozac for depression, it only treated the depression—not the mania. This is why those eleven months during which Heather was placed on medications—first for ADHD, then for depression—were when her episodes of mania intensified.

Her medications were contributing to her increased rage rather than their intended improvement. Although bipolar is highly treatable, there is not a cure for it today. The greatest obstacle to continuous, successful treatment of this illness is evident in the on-again, off-again cycle by the patient with medications.

Because medication greatly reduces, or in some cases eliminates, the manic-depressive episodes, the patient starts to feel as if she does not need it any longer. Her reasoning goes, *I'm doing fine, so I don't need my meds*. But once the person goes off the medication, her episodes of mania or depression resurface.

She's Home!

Heather's return home was a joyous occasion for my family. Yet it was difficult finding our way back to a comfortable routine. For so many years we did not have a "normal" life, so we all were trying to find our way again.

I could tell that Heather was different. She seemed more relaxed and comfortable. She took pleasure in the simple things of life and did not get stressed out about things that would have overwhelmed her in the past.

The first two months home we were given the resources of family counseling to help Heather and our family with the transition. Bruce and Sallie, both family social workers, came to our home two nights a week to assist us in developing an in-home treatment plan to manage Heather's illness.

Until returning home, Heather had the structure and external controls that the RTC provided. If she were to successfully stay at home and learn to live with her illness, she needed to gain insight into the volatility of her extreme moods and know how to manage them.

The Chinese have a saying: "To conquer the beast, one must first make it a friend." This saying aptly applies to what it takes to live with bipolar. Heather and our family first had to understand the symptoms of bipolar and then develop ways to prevent further relapses of extreme mood swings.

It is said that bipolar is a family illness. I can certainly attest to that. This illness wreaks havoc on the patient's perception of how she feels about herself and her ability to trust her judgments about those closest to her. This is why helping Heather can be so difficult. What I may try to provide by way of love and comfort to Heather, she may see as a threat. For this reason, developing an in-home treatment plan was critical. Heather said to me at the end of her stay at the RTC, "Mom, don't ever let me get that bad again."

Once she was finally diagnosed and properly treated, Heather could see just how deep the despair once was. She realized that the deeper she got into despair, the harder it was to dig her way out. For some, it becomes so deep they can't find their way back, and they resort to the only option they see available—suicide.

As Heather's mother, my focus is to make sure that she has the love and support she needs in order to learn how to manage this illness. The crucial role a family plays for their loved one suffering with bipolar is evident in many studies.

Over the past decade, several studies have found that patients hospitalized for bipolar more often climb back on the emotional roller coaster if they encounter a lot of daily stress.

In contrast, a new investigation finds that people treated for an episode of mania or depression recover within about eight months if they have supportive family and friends. As Heather's parents, Steve and I try to provide an environment that stresses the importance of Heather's medications and minimizes the stress to which she is exposed, in order to help her deal with the illness effectively.

Sallie, a six-foot-tall woman, fascinated us all with her tales of basketball. Bruce's sport was baseball. They both had different skills that helped us with the transition. With their assistance, we devised a plan to help Heather learn to live productively with this illness.

Heather's treatment plan consisted of taking her medications on a regular basis, getting adequate rest, and surrounding herself with family and friends who can be her barometer when things are not going well. They may ask her, "Are you okay?" or "Do you need help?" or the question she hates most, "Are you taking your medications?"

Heather did fine the first two months home. She quickly got caught up with her school studies. Her brothers were not such quick learners as she is; it was slightly annoying for them that she was able to pick up on her school work where she left off without much effort.

Our family was whole again and I prayed every day for it to stay that way. I focused my energy on maintaining a positive attitude about what the future had in store for us and to let go of the past.

The visits with Bruce and Sallie were helpful because they provided a stabilizing force for Heather, but when they stopped, Heather was not as diligent about taking her medications.

I began to suspect that she was not taking them because her moods were becoming more extreme again. Since lithium works only when the patient maintains a specific blood-serum level, missing one or two doses periodically can render the medication ineffective, thus causing the relapse of Heather's extreme mood swings.

I had to continually remind Heather to take her medications. But she was not always receptive to my warnings. After another week, I called Sallie to get some advice. Sallie reminded me that Heather would need me to reinforce her plan, and if needed, I was to give Heather her medications each day (this worked only if Heather swallowed the pills as opposed to hiding them in her cheek and spitting them out later).

I soon became a pest to Heather about her medications, but when she got annoyed with me I gently reminded her that she once asked me not to let her get real bad again. This reminder worked for a while, but within another month Heather was skipping most of her medication. Just as I was preparing to approach Heather about her pills she came to me and said, "Mom, I hate having to take my medication."

I put my arm on her shoulder and said, "Heather, I know you hate having to take medication every day, but it is important.

Without it we all suffer from your violent mood swings. I hope some-day you will be free of your medication, but right now you need it."

She obviously did not like my answer when she said, "What if I just decide to stop taking it?" She emphasized, "You can't make me take it."

I responded, "No Heather, I can't make you take it, but your father and I will not allow our family be controlled again by this ill-ness."

I knew the implication of her words so I added, "We can't control your will to take the medication but we can control the kind of environment we live in and we will not live like that again. So I hope you choose to take your medication."

I tried to say my words with a delicate balance of compassion and firmness.

I said, "Heather, we love you and want you here, not in a hos-pital or an institution. I know that what you have to deal with is a big burden, but please don't let this illness take away your happiness."

She looked at me intently and I saw her eyes flinch. I said, "You are stronger than you give yourself credit for."

I was certain she did not like what I had to say but she seemed to reflect upon it. After that, she was diligent in taking her medica-tions, and I rarely had to remind her.

Heather did not start back into the public school right away. She went back full time into the outpatient-partial program for the remainder of her seventh grade. She continued without any problems. At the beginning of eighth grade, she was placed back in the local public school full time. Going back into the public school was a major mile-stone for Heather. There Heather still received some special-education services but spent most of her time in the mainstream classes.

It was amazing to see her progress in six short months. Life became very routine and normal for Heather and our family. What once was a life of immense daily struggle now became one of hope and joy.

As Heather continued to improve, she was legally released back into our custody. In February 1997, Heather was no longer a ward of the state. Not one year had passed and we had gone from the darkness back to the light. For the next two and a half years, we experienced great pleasure in living very "normal" lives and reestablishing bonds that had once been injured. After so many years of living in the shadow of fear, it was wonderful to be able to reclaim our lives.

February 22, 1997

*Steve and I have custody of Heather again!
I thought this day would never come. It is
wonderful to have her back with her family
where she belongs.*

Part Six:
Slowly Back into the Light

Mania's Intoxicating Grip

I would love to end the story here and say that we all lived happily ever after. Sadly, Heather struggles with the on-again, off-again cycles with the medication.

In ninth grade, Heather stopped taking her medications. She, like countless other successfully–treated persons with bipolar, fell into the belief, *I'm doing fine, I don't need my medications.*

Initially, she would take her meds one day and skip the next or take it one week and skip the next. The result of her on-again, off-again cycle with her medications caused her to relapse into cycles of mania and depression.

Heather's relapse was not something I wanted to deal with. I simply wanted to live our lives without the burden and interruption from her illness. I soon learned that we were just beginning the long road to stability.

Over the next year, from early 1999 to March 2000, Heather's mood swings became a significant interruption in our lives again. At age fourteen, her mood swings were different than what she experienced as a young child. Her cycles of depression or mania were now more episodic in nature with a longer period of "normalcy" in between.

By April 2000, Heather's behavior became severe enough that she was, once again, placed into the custody of the state and put into a treatment center.

This time Heather was placed in a center for girls ranging in age from twelve to nineteen. The center was nestled in a scenic country setting that looked nothing like an institution. Cottages abutted the woods. Wildlife of all varieties often wandered the land surrounding the cottages. Deer, turkeys, and rabbits frequented the outskirts of the cottages.

Though it was still a lock-down facility, it sure beat the cold, sterile walls and barred windows of the first center Heather was in. I held on to the hope that Heather's surroundings would aid in her healing.

After six months, Heather began writing to deal with her emotions and separation from her family. She, like I, found refuge in putting into words the emotions that can be so overwhelming at times. One day, as she was waiting to go outside for therapy, she wrote the following essay:

JUST HANG ON

You know that feeling you get when you take a deep breath of fresh air, that sense of being free? Well, not completely free, after all, we are locked up. But who says we can't still enjoy life and our surroundings?

There are so many beautiful trees outside and the turkeys are funny enough to make even the deepest pain just a little bit less. The occasional deer makes you stand in awe, and the stray cats and cute little bunnies make you just want to pick them up and pet them.

After a little while, life gradually gets a little better because these things can make me happy when I'm sad and laugh when I'm mad.

I love that time when the staff let you out to walk between the buildings and the air fills my lungs, air that hasn't been re circulated over and over, always adding a few funky smells each time.

These little things are a reminder for me to just hang on. I'll be out soon and then I'll be able to take that breath of fresh air just about whenever I want.

Heather Byers
September 2000

Because Heather was treated and released after only five months in the previous treatment center, I went into this stay with the belief that she would be home within five or six months. After six months, I began to see the error of my thinking.

Life can be challenging enough for a fourteen-year-old. Add the challenges of dealing with a mood disorder, and it became painfully obvious that Heather needed longer treatment. As each month passed, the agony of Heather's absence was more difficult to bear.

After more than ten months at the treatment center, I was becoming frustrated with Heather's lack of progress. Then the next week, during a visit Heather said to me, "Mom, I have a confession to make."

Immediately an alarm went off in my head. Steeling myself for what she had to say, I nervously responded, "What?"

She said, "I've been cutting myself."

Heather described how she hid a razor blade from the staff, and at night, alone in her bedroom, she cut her thighs and stomach with the razor.

She said this with such steadiness in her voice and calm on her face that it took a few minutes for my mind to register her words. Trying not to look as scared as I was, I asked her, "Why do you do this?"

She said, "The emotional pain is so bad that sometimes the physical pain makes it go away for a while."

The impact of her words hit me like a blow to the head. Tears immediately filled my eyes.

In anguish I responded, "I wish I could understand what you were going through."

Heather looked me squarely in the eyes and said, "No, Mom, you don't. I wouldn't wish these feelings on anyone."

I held her hands in mine, and we talked a little longer. Her confession hit me with mixed emotions. I was reminded, once again, just how destructive this illness is and how hard it can be to stabilize.

I also realized how hard it was for Heather to admit her self-destructive behavior. I took her confession as a good sign that she was seeking help instead of trying to hide her pain.

I AM angry
I WONDER why
I HEAR voices in my head telling me what to do
I SEE nothing
I WANT something more

I PRETEND everything's not
I FEEL overwhelming pain
I TOUCH what I wish it were
I WORRY that I've hurt them so
I CRY because I don't know what to do
I AM lonely

I UNDERSTAND being here is for the best
I SAY I'll move on
I DREAM of a day when all is not
I TRY to see a future
I HOPE this will all go away
I AM scared

Heather Byers
December 2000

Just after dinner on a Sunday evening in February 2001, the phone rang. I answered it and was greeted by Joanna, Heather's case manager at the treatment center. I could not think of any good reason why Joanna would be calling us at 6:00 p.m. on a Sunday evening.

Joanna said, "Leslie, Heather is in the hospital."

"Oh my God, what is wrong?" I cried.

Joanna responded, "Heather took a bottle of Tylenol."

I tried to speak but the words caught in my throat. I held the phone to my ear and after a few seconds Joanna said, "I do not know how she is now but when she left here by ambulance almost thirty minutes ago she was fairly lethargic."

Joanna told me which hospital Heather had been taken to. I put the phone on the cradle and stood there a moment, trying to collect my thoughts.

I called out to Steve from the kitchen. When I told him what happened, we decided he would stay with the boys while I went to the hospital. We did not want to alarm the boys until we knew how serious Heather's condition was.

I rushed to the hospital and upon entering asked to see Heather. The nurse told me, "I'm sorry—you cannot see your daughter. You are not her legal guardian."

I yelled, "What do you mean I cannot see my daughter?" Just then, one of the staff from the treatment center who escorted Heather came to my side and nodded to the nurse. The nurse then escorted me into the treatment room.

I was not prepared for what I saw as I entered the treatment room. Heather's face was bloated to twice its size and she looked like she had been beaten. That is because the blood vessels and capillaries in her face and neck had burst during the violent retching as they pumped her stomach. She also had black blotches on her face and hands from the charcoal they made her ingest to absorb the poison in her system.

I stood in the corner, trying to remain calm, as they continued working on Heather. After a few more minutes, the doctor finished and left the rest to the nurses.

Heather turned her head my way and our eyes met. I saw a flash of anguish cross her eyes before she turned her head away.

Within a few minutes, the last nurse finished. As she turned to leave the room, she told me I could go to Heather.

I walked toward her, uncertain as to what to say or do. The mixture of emotions I felt was confusing. Before I could say anything, Heather put her arms out to me and said, "Mom, I'm so sorry, I did not mean to hurt you."

I held her. The red blotches on her face deepened as she sobbed in my arms.

She said, "Mom, I will never do that again. I saw in your eyes the kind of hell you and Dad would have to live with if I killed myself."

Now I was the one sobbing in her arms.

Heather was admitted to the hospital for observation in the surgical ward. I was not happy about that, but there were no psychiatric beds in that hospital, or any within the entire city. After three days, she returned to the treatment center.

Heather continued her treatment and spent another eighteen months in the residential treatment center. On July 1, 2002, she came home to her family once again.

What We Now Know

There were many times I felt such an overwhelming sense of grief that Heather has spent so much of her childhood away from her family. With the two stays in a residential treatment center, Heather had spent nearly three years away from her family.

One Sunday morning during Heather's second stay at the treatment center, as Steve and I sat at the table, reading the newspaper, my thoughts turned to Heather.

Without warning, the tears came. Steve looked over at me and asked me why I was crying. I replied, "I miss Heather so much. This is not what we had planned for our family."

Steve said, "No, Leslie, this is not what we had planned, but we have to do what's best under the circumstances. That's all we can do. If this is Heather's best chance of learning how to manage this illness—to have a chance to lead a productive adult life—then we have to be strong for her."

As hard as it was to admit, I knew that Steve was right. We always felt that if we could get an answer to Heather's mental and behavioral problems as soon as possible, she had a better chance to turn her life around early.

Heather's first time in the treatment center, at age ten, was for diagnosis. The second time, at age fourteen, was to enable her to learn how to live with her illness.

Parenthood was never promised to be an easy job. As a mother, I so desperately wanted to make Heather's pain go away by making excuses for her behavior. But Steve and I knew that if we were to be instrumental in enabling Heather to battle this illness on her own in preparation for her adult years, we sometimes had to stand back and watch her struggle. That is not easy for a parent to do.

I once heard the parable of a man who noticed a butterfly struggling to untangle itself while trying to come out of its cocoon. The man, thinking he was helping, cut the butterfly loose—only to discover two days later that the butterfly had died because it needed to struggle through the cocoon in order to develop the strength to endure its new life as a butterfly.

This is what we, Heather's parents, have to do—to let her struggle with the help from her family and God's loving strength in order to become strong in her new life. This tough love is a lot easier said than done.

Through this experience I learned a lot. What I know today will enable my family to live our lives, in spite of, and because of, the challenges presented by this illness.

Heather still battles the "bad days" when her lithium level gets out of balance. But the degree of difficulty is lessened with each maturing discovery.

Although bipolar more often manifests itself in the adolescent or adult years, doctors now know it can begin in early childhood. Doctors have reason to believe that bipolar sets up a pattern in the brain that can repeat itself; therefore, the earlier the intervention, the earlier this pattern can be broken. That is why early detection and intervention programs are so critical.

Unfortunately, there is not a universal childhood screening and diagnosis program in place for mental illness. As a result, too many children and families suffer for years before getting the right help. I remember shortly after Heather's diagnosis came in 1996, after eight years of living with the effects of untreated mental illness, how remarkably full and healthy our lives had become again. I wanted to keep it that way, so I began doing research on this illness. What I learned amazed me. I remember saying to Steve several times, "This all makes sense, I feel like I am putting a puzzle together. I wish we knew then what we know now."

I learned that the combination of the hereditary influence from my mother's side of the family, the traumatic impact of Heather's iron overdose at sixteen months of age, and the early behavioral problems Heather exhibited are what the Surgeon General referred to in his annual report in 2001 as "biological markers."

It stated, "Increasingly, research has shown that a number of biological markers that can be identified early in a child's life have predictive power for the development of future problems. Unfortunately, these problems tend to go unrecognized or untreated and most children do not receive treatment early in life unless the problems are severe."

This research clearly correlates with Heather's manifestation and symptoms and is a good example of the need for establishing a national, universal child-screening program.

Being diagnosed with bipolar does not have to mean that the person's life has less meaning or fulfillment. It does mean having to deal with adversity made more difficult because mental illness is one of the illnesses least accepted by society. Mental illness is, sadly, still treated as a second-class disease.

It is my hope that, in the future, there will be greater acceptance and understanding by society that mental illnesses are real illnesses that have a highly successful treatment rate, and that the patient, especially a child, should be afforded every opportunity to receive treatment.

There is still much stigma and ignorance associated with mental illness. The prevailing attitude by society is that bad behavior in children must mean bad parenting. This stigma caused undue stress for Steve and me in trying to find an answer to Heather's extreme behavior. Far too often, we were targeted by the professionals as the reason for Heather's problems.

There is still great ignorance in the special-education system, and disparity within the insurance industry, when it comes to understanding and aiding children with mental illness. I hope the future will see improvement in these systems.

I cringe to think of what would have happened to Heather

if she had been placed in jail as a result of her threat against me. In jail I'm certain Heather would have only deteriorated, or worse, become criminal. There are far too many adolescents—and adults—in jail whose behavior is a result of untreated mental illness.

As Heather continues down the road to recovery, my family is blessed with a great abundance of faith, hope, and love. Faith that God's plan is present in our lives and that He is using this illness for His good; hope for continued recovery; and unending love for one another.

Recovery, unfortunately, does not mean a cure. For me, recovery defines the point at which this illness is no longer the essence of Heather's existence. It is also a time when our lives are reclaimed and our family is reestablished.

There was a long time when I doubted that we would ever find the light of recovery, which I now realize is a life-long process.

A wise doctor once passed along this great advice to persons with bipolar on the road to recovery: "Gather what you need in yourself for the journey, pack a first-aid kit, and take people you trust with you."

I think this is good advice for any challenge we may struggle with in life.

Part Seven:
The Future's Bright Light

A Family's Love

Thomas la Mance once said, "Life is what happens to us while we are making other plans."

The plans Steve and I had for our family did not include having to deal with a child afflicted with bipolar. We knew raising children would not be an easy job, but the challenges brought upon us by Heather's illness often left us dumbfounded.

Symptoms of Heather's illness emerged in her earliest childhood and changed our lives forever. Through the eight-year period from manifestation to diagnosis, the darkness, at times, seemed as if it would never end.

The mystery surrounding Heather's abnormal and uncontrollable behavior was frustrating, especially because Steve and I expected to be able to shield our child from such pain, even if it meant taking on the burden ourselves. But Steve and I were inadequately equipped to do so. So we turned to our faith to give us the strength we needed to sustain us. With every step into the darkness of the unknown, we somehow came back into the light—the light of faith, hope, and love.

Our lives were once dominated by Heather's struggles—which began with the manifestation of the symptoms at a very early age. Her moods evolved into an unrelenting series of episodes of depression and mania that progressed from one to the next until the realization hit that we, her parents, could not fully help her.

In order for Heather to get the right treatment, we were forced to relinquish custody of her to the state. No parent should have to do such a thing just because his or her child suffers from a mental illness.

Unfortunately, this practice is a common one throughout the United States. Although thirteen states have laws prohibiting child welfare agencies from requiring parents and other caregivers to relinquish custody to access services for their children with mental illness, thirty-seven states still practice it. Those states that bar custody relinquishment are Colorado, Connecticut, Idaho, Indiana, Iowa, Maine, Massachusetts, Minnesota, North Dakota, Oregon, Rhode Island, Vermont, and Wisconsin. It is my hope that someday this practice will be abolished across the entire country.

With God's grace, we finally made it to the eventual turning point that enabled discovery, recovery, and healing to take place. At our worst moments, there were times when I dreaded hearing the phone ring for fear it was the call that said Heather had succeeded in one of her suicide attempts.

Finally, with the proper diagnosis, the right medical treatment, and therapy, Heather is still learning a powerful discovery of acceptance and self-discipline that will enable her to lead a productive life.

I know this illness can tear a family apart, if you let it. But if I can share a message with others who are struggling with a family member or friend suffering from the symptoms of bipolar, my message would be, "Don't ever give up!"

In the dark times, Steve and I held on to a strong faith that if we could find the right diagnosis early, then recovery and healing would be easier and more sustainable.

Bipolar is highly treatable. The biggest challenge for those suffering from it is getting the right diagnosis. I have heard of many who have suffered from this illness for decades before finally getting a diagnosis, and others who still are seeking diagnosis. For still others, it did not come in time to save them from the lows that led to suicide.

Bipolar is not curable, but it is treatable. Unless God gives us a cure—which I pray for every day—Heather will have to manage this illness for the rest of her life.

For right now, God's answer to our prayers is to enable Heather and our family to live with this illness in order to lead a healthy, productive life. This is what I accept. The pain seemed unbearable at times, and pain will take you on a journey. But on that journey there will be hope.

I went into motherhood with the attitude that I had nothing to learn from my children and everything to teach them. Boy, was I wrong! I have learned so much from my children. Dealing with Heather's illness helped me to learn how to deal with adversity without becoming bitter and mean. Seeing Heather become a mature, caring individual, in spite of her obstacles, is an inspiration to me.

George F. Will, syndicated news columnist, once eloquently described parenting when he wrote, "Biologically, adults produce children. Spiritually, children produce adults. Most of us do not grow up until we have helped children do so. Thus do the generations form a braided cord."

I know many adults who could not have handled this kind of adversity with the amount of grace and dignity that Heather has shown. Having to deal with this illness can truly be a blessing rather than a curse, but only if you choose to make it so. I believe Heather has.

My Faith

In the Bible, the book of Job is a powerful story. Job was a godly man who lived a good life and was blessed with much happiness and riches. One day Satan approached God and accused Job of loving God only because of Job's riches. Satan said to God, "If I take away everything Job holds dearly, I bet he won't follow you anymore."

God agreed to allow Satan to take away Job's wealth and family—certain that Job would continue to love him. When all of Job's children died and his riches were taken away, Job turned to God in his grief to give him strength.

Angered that this did not cause Job to curse God, Satan caused purulent sores to form all over Job's body. The sores caused great pain and discomfort but Job still kept his faith—even when his wife asked him to denounce God.

Job's pain and suffering continued. One day, three of Job's friends came to visit and tried to cheer him up. The friends believed that wealth and happiness are blessings from God and since Job was suffering, they were convinced he did something wrong to earn God's disfavor. Job argued vehemently that he did nothing wrong and his friends begged Job to repent from his sins.

After much arguing, neither was able to prove the other right. After a while, the friends stopped arguing and left.

Alone and in constant pain, Job begged God to give him an answer for his suffering. Many times he cried out, "God, why must I suffer? I've done nothing wrong!"

Job never did understand why he had to suffer. Many times he felt bitter, but he never rejected God. Finally, God appeared to

Job, but not to explain the reason for Job's suffering. Instead, God made Job realize that we cannot understand the things he does. I, like Job, have come to live the Bible passage, "Trust in the LORD with all your heart and lean not on your own understanding" (Proverbs 3:5).

God criticized Job for arguing so much with his friends when Job knew so little. But because Job remained a faithful servant, God rewarded him by making him twice as wealthy and providing him with many more children.

I, like Job, went through the same cycle of anger and confusion at what appeared to be God's abandonment toward my family. I believed if I just prayed harder or worked harder, all our problems would go away.

I often reasoned, "Surely I can fix this."

I was bitter for a long time, but deep down, I knew God was still there. Finally, when all my efforts failed, I learned to be content in not finding all the answers to our quest and to let God work his plans for my family.

Job suffered for a while, and upon a timetable accorded by God, he was delivered from his affliction. Job, through his humanness, despaired just like I did. Through his despair, he clung firmly to the faith that God's plan was in his life.

There are days I do not know if I can take much more. I want healing for my daughter's chronic illness—and I want it now. But until then, I will remain faithful and hopeful.

To sustain that faith and hope, I turn to the verse in Hebrews 11:1-2: "Now Faith is being sure of what we hope for and certain of what we do not see."

Epilogue

Melt Away the Rage

So many times I have asked myself, "Why did Heather become afflicted with this illness?" Although there may never be a conclusive answer to this question, the variables presented in Heather's case appear to fit like pieces of the bipolar puzzle.

The history of bipolar on my mother's side of the family and the traumatic early experience of Heather's drug overdose add up to a deadly combination of biological and environmental ingredients that, combined, doctors believe can trigger this illness.

As Heather's mother, I can only share my feelings and hopes for her. As much as I may try, I cannot truly know what Heather struggles with or feels in moments of mania or depression.

Many times I wished I could know what Heather was thinking. When she was in a rage, what was really going through her mind? Without understanding her wants and needs, I felt helpless to know how to help.

One day in the early winter of 1999, I received a poem from a friend. She received this poem from her daughter, who was living in a mental-health institution at the time. Her daughter gave the poem to her mother with the message that read, "Mom, this poem expresses my feelings better than I can."

I read the poem and was awestruck by the depth of awareness it presented to me. Every now and then I read it again to remind myself of Heather's struggles and I ask myself, *Do I provide the warmth of one who can melt away the rage?*

YOU ASK ME WHAT I WANT

You ask me what I want, in those times when you attempt,
To be the type of healer who does not show contempt
For the dreams and aspirations, I hold buried deep inside,
Covered by the illness, I no longer try to hide.

Others do not talk of wants, they lecture about needs,
They then appear to be upset, when their plans for me do not succeed,
I know some truly think they have my best interest at heart,
When they invalidate my visions and pick my dreams apart.

I want you to know my illness cannot reveal the wonder that is me,
It captures not my essence, my yearning to be free,
From haunting voices and disjointed thoughts, nagging in my brain,
Free to be a person, whom illness cannot explain.

I want a home where I feel at ease, not pressured to conform,
Where I can do the things I like, versus having to perform,
The tasks and goals the staff decides everyone should do,
Like cooking meals for groups of twelve, or being in bed by two.

I want to talk with others, without seeing the ashen look upon their face,
When they learn of my disorder, got to get out of this place.
I want a job where I fit in, and make a decent wage,
I want to feel the warmth of one who can melt away the rage.

I want the things that you want, to be respected and affirmed,
I want the things that you want, to have personhood confirmed.
I want the things that you want, to laugh and to belong,
To feel the sun upon my face, to sing a joyful song.

I want others to know I did not choose to be this way,
And sometimes I am not so sure, I can take another day.
I want to feel needed, to break out of patient roles,
And if you hear and feel my words, you'll help me reach my goals.

©1992 Wally Kisthardt

Sources Consulted

Patty Duke and Gloria Hochman. *A Brilliant Madness: Living with Manic Depressive Illness.* New York: Bantam Books, 1992.

Penelope Parker. *The Road Back: A Patient's-Eye View of Thirty Years in the Psychiatric Syndrome.* New York: Vantage Press, 1997.

Kay Redfield Jamison. *An Unquiet Mind: A Memoir of Moods and Madness.* New York: Alfred A. Knopf, 1995.

_____. *Manic Depressive Illness.* New York: Oxford University Press, 1990.

E. Fuller Torrey, et al. *Schizophrenia and Manic-Depressive Disorders: The Biological Roots of Mental Illness as Revealed by the Landmark Studies of Identical Twins.* New York: BasicBooks, 1994

Michelle McKinney Hammond. *Get Over It and On With It: How to Get Up When Life Knocks You Down.* Colorado: Waterbook Press, 2002.

Hagop S. Akiskal et al. *The Relationship of Personality to Affective Disorders.* Archives of General Psychiatry, 1983 (July): 801-809.

Department of Health and Human Services in collaboration with the Department of Education and Department of Justice. *Report of the Surgeon General's Conference on Children's Mental Health: A National Action Agenda.* 2001 (January): 21–23.